Professional Suicide

Professional Suicide

A Survival Kit for You and Your Job

Donald W. Cole

McGraw-Hill Book Company

New York	Singapore
St. Louis	Johannesburg
San Francisco	Mexico
Auckland	Hamburg
Bogotá	Panama
Saõ Paulo	Paris
London	Sydney
Madrid	Montreal
New Delhi	Tokyo

Library of Congress Cataloging in Publication Data
Cole, Donald W
    Professional Suicide—A Survival Kit for You and Your Job

    Bibliography: p.
    Includes index.
    1. Job stress. I. Title.
HF5548.85.C64 1980   658.3'82   80-10728
ISBN 0–07–011697–0

1234567890   MUMU   8987654321

The editors for this book were William Newton and Ann Gray,
the designer was Mark E. Safran, and the production supervisor
was Paul A. Malchow. It was set in Garamond by Datapage.

It was printed and bound by The Murray Printing Company.

Dedicated to Pierce Angell without whose insights, support, and understanding this study would never have been initiated; to Norma, Susan, Wheeler, Michael, David, and Erik; and to all those involved in the study who so freely shared their thoughts and feelings with me.

Contents

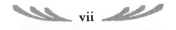

Preface

There are a number of different kinds of suicide. There is physical suicide in which people die bodily, there is psychological suicide in which they die emotionally, and there is professional suicide in which they die professionally. This book is about the problem of professional suicide.

I have defined professional suicide as the process in which creative, aggressive, well-educated, highly intelligent people suddenly, over a relatively brief period, take steps that can only lead their careers with organizations in a negative direction. They do this in many ways:

1. Some suddenly quit their jobs for others far beneath their capabilities.

2. Some become disruptive and do things for which they must know they will be fired.

3. Some suddenly "retire" on the job and work with minimal effort.

4. Others, caught up in the day-to-day crises of the job, do not keep up technically and gradually become obsolete.

5. Others develop psychosomatic complaints of backaches, headaches, and ulcers.

6. And some, told to slow down by their doctors, are not able to and seem headed for physical suicide.

This book describes a process that appears to be occurring with increasing frequency in many organizations and includes findings from study of this little-recognized problem done within a major U.S. corporation, with suggestions for possible solutions.

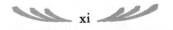

Chapter 1 lists the most common routes to professional suicide, then introduces the major categories of organizational problems that provoke a suicidal response. The requirements for a mutually beneficial company-employee relationship are set forth, followed by a brief background of organizational attempts to create a psychologically healthier work environment.

Chapter 2 traces the historical evolution of various management philosphies and the factors that influenced them. The relationship between the organization's philosophy of management and professional suicide is clarified, and an examination of management policy is recommended and a new direction proposed that would foster the correction of the problems.

Chapter 3 traces the characteristic path of professional suicide and the various stages through which individuals move toward it. Chapters 4 and 5 discuss specific factors in individuals and in the environment that contributes to the problem. Chapter 6 describes relevant research on people and on animals to help us better understand theoretically the process of professional suicide. Chapter 7 discusses the antidote to the problem. Chapter 8 summarizes findings and recommendations; and the Appendixes describe in detail the five phases of the study that inspired this book, the characteristics of creative talent, one organization's reward system, and a group exercise clarifying "the manager's dilemma."

This is not a book about the way management intended things to happen or a book about the way management in retrospect thought things happened; it is a book about the way people within an organization saw things happen. The situation studied and the findings are just as valid today as they were when the study was made.

Donald W. Cole

Acknowledgments

This study could not have been made without the help of many people. Special recognition should go to the organization within which this study was undertaken and to those in managerial control: first, for being enlightened enough to recognize the problem; second, for being willing to initiate a study of the problem; and third, for allowing the study to be completed in spite of the criticism directed at the existing philosophy of management and at a number of organizational practices.

I would especially like to express my appreciation to the many people willing to spend time in reading at least some portion of the drafts of this material. These include: Pierce Angell, Ben Barish, Dick Beckhard, Al Bochner, M.D., Rae Conway, Burt Crobaugh, Charles Donahue, Dr. Frank Friedlander, Skip Giddings, Dr. Nathan Grundstein, Bob Hauserman, Frank Jobes, Dr. Bill Johnson, Larry Jones, Bob Kenyon, Dr. Elaine Kepner, Harley King, Al Koestal, Vic Kovacik, Bob Landies, Pat Lawlor, Dr. Al Nemy, Dr. Howard Parad, Jim Rechin, Gene Richter, Jack Skievaski, Dr. Jim Skinner, Dr. Cameron Smith, Fernley Smith, Nelson Spoth, Dr. Herman Stein, Ed Taylor, Art Thompson, Bob Tomasko, Ray Whitmore, Dr. Tom Wickes, Dick Williams, Jim Wise, Dr. Donald Wolfe, Don Worley and Dr. Richard Wynveen. Dr. C. C. VanVechten was especially helpful in criticizing the early drafts of this book.

Although I am grateful for their many comments and suggestions, the conclusions in this report and any inaccuracies are solely my own responsibility. It was, however, reassuring to me to know that many others saw the same organizational problems I saw and

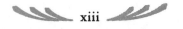

to know that my conclusions were not unique to me but common to them and to their experience also.

Professional Suicide

one

The Problem

For every manager who succeeds in business today, dozens are left by the wayside. Thousands of potentially first-rate managers and executives find themselves committing professional suicide and don't know what they can do to reverse the process. Managers see good employees deteriorating and becoming less useful to the organization and don't know how to change this trend. The deterioration of these talented individuals is manifested in seven ways:

1.   They quit their jobs for other jobs far beneath their abilities.

2.   They become disruptive and do things for which (management assumes) they must know they will be fired.

3.   They stop working to capacity and gradually "retire on the job."

4.   They get caught up in a flurry of daily crises, do not keep up with the rapidly changing technology, and over a period of time find themselves outmoded and obsolete.

5.   They develop classic psychosomatic complaints, such as headaches, ulcers, backaches, and so on. (Alcoholism, readily identified by the community as a form of professional suicide, was infrequently found among the group of managers, engineers, and scientists studied, possibly because individuals who try to solve their problems with alcohol are not promoted to this level, or at least have enough experience in masking their problem so that they are rarely found out.)

6.   They are placed, after having been highly productive in the past, in jobs where, for various reasons, they are grossly un-

derutilized. Unable to resolve the problem with their bosses and unwilling to quit, they quietly begin to deteriorate with the constant feeling of being regarded as inadequate by their peers.

7.   They are unable to slow down or lose weight or quit smoking and seem headed for actual physical suicide.

Investigators and observers have suspected these suicidal trends for years. The tendency for some people in some organizations to initiate the process of professional suicide was confirmed by a unique, in-depth study conducted within a major U.S. corporation. The details of this study and how it was conducted can be found in the Appendix. But more important right now is to consider the conclusions of the study, which may apply to many people you supervise today. They may also apply to you. In either case, knowledge of these conclusions and recognition of the symptoms of professional suicide will enable you to plan corrective action now—before it is too late.

Later we will examine each problem uncovered by the study and suggest ways to interpret it—and to take preventive action. But first we will categorize the major problems as follows:

1.   Unclear, unrealistic expectations and nebulous situations. Many managers were never quite sure where they stood with the organization and what was expected of them. Many were waiting for "management" to come up with answers, while management waited for them to do the same.

2.   A management philosophy of "running lean," which often meant never enough resources to do the job right, but always enough to do it over. There was extensive use of "voluntary" overtime; 60- to 70-hour work weeks were not uncommon.

3.   A management philosophy based on subordinate commitment, meaning that advancement was based not so much on the technical excellence of the job done (which was poorly defined at best), as on the effort and commitment demonstrated in doing it.

4.   Poor planning and fatigue. When people are tired enough over a long enough period of time, they respond only to crises. The result for this organization was that its employees were totally

consumed in crisis interventions and neglected orderly constructive efforts to plan for and reduce future crises.

5. Poor communication and a particular reluctance to advise people where they stood with respect to job security and promotion within the organization. Much effort was directed toward placating people with platitudes that left them unaware of their actual positions.

6. Neglect or fear to communicate plans, causing people to grossly misunderstand the organization, what it was trying to accomplish, and where they fit in.

7. Too little recognition or even awareness of the good work being done, and a general preoccupation with problems past and present. This did little to strengthen the individual confidence necessary for the difficult tasks which needed doing.

8. In several instances, a great concern for keeping people happy, at the expense of glossing over their problems for as long as possible and then resolving them by sudden transfer from one area to another. (This transfer was accompanied by praise, leaving the individual frustrated and the larger organization misled about what had really happened.)

9. Responsibility for getting organizational tasks accomplished was placed on committed "charismatic" leaders who would get results with minimal use of organizational resources. Such persons, once found, were in great demand, and were given successively more difficult problems to solve (usually with almost no opportunity for development or formal organizational help). When they finally failed, their capabilities were "reevaluated," and eventually organizational hopes were transferred to new personalities.

10. Although management pinned great hopes on committed charismatic leaders, their peers and the organization at large frequently saw them as threats. With organizational goals poorly defined, organizational relationships poorly communicated, and authority to do a job largely withheld, it became more and more difficult for such leaders to obtain voluntary cooperation from peers already very busy with other things. It was also commonly assumed that by giving too much help to a peer, one might end

up subordinate to that peer. When, in addition, organizational rewards seemed to be coming no closer and the joy of task accomplishment was being felt less frequently (because of growing organizational resistance or mounting fatigue, or both), it would have been surprising if some leaders had not looked for alternative opportunities to use their energies.

What makes these conclusions all the more devastating is that typical managers already involved in the suicide process voiced the following opinions:

"I want to do a good job. I am committed. But I simply cannot figure out what management really wants from me."

"I have never had a bona fide, constructive performance appraisal. No one has made it clear what is expected of me."

"I'd like to talk to someone about my personal frustrations, my feelings of at times being irrelevant to this organization; but there is no one who I feel I can really trust."

Obviously, when potentially capable people in an organization begin to act against their own best interests, responsible management should take steps to remove destructive conditions and to establish relationships conducive to profitable performance. The requirements for an effective organization include:

1.   A purpose: Creative talent must have a well-defined purpose in order to be used effectively. Vague concepts such as "make a profit and grow" are not adequate.

2.   A plan: Creative talent cannot be used effectively without a well-thought-out plan for its use.

3.   A team: Creative talent is most effectively used in concert with others toward common organizational objectives.

4.   A periodic evaluation of results: Creative people need to feel some sense of accomplishment, which is difficult without a periodic evaluation of results. Help is also needed periodically to focus energy on organizationally relevant objectives.

5.   Training programs: Creative talent requires regular training to maintain skills and develop new ones. It is especially important to develop interpersonal and communication skills.

6.   Frequent reclarification of the psychological contract and the

rules of the game: Nothing discourages good people faster than the discovery that the psychological contract and the rules of the game have been changed without their knowledge.

7. Periodic release from pressure: Only with regularly scheduled release from severe pressure can talent remain creative and energetic. A two-week vacation once a year is not adequate for people in high-pressure positions.

8. Maintenance of system anxiety at a reasonable level: It is extremely difficult in highly stressful, anxiety-provoking environments to maintain the objective, innovative atmosphere so necessary for creative people to do their best. The maintenance of too high an anxiety state in an organization eventually leads to immature problem solving.

9. Regular evaluation of organization talent and work force planning: Effective use of creative talent requires periodic evaluation of the organization's work force mix and some direction for those who may be spending their energies in organizationally irrelevant ways.

10. A program for organization development: Organizations, like machines, become obsolete, and there must be mechanisms for periodically diagnosing them and improving their effectiveness. Creative people who find themselves spending too much time and energy fighting obsolete organizational structures eventually develop other plans for themselves or become involved in some form of professional suicide.

Historical Background

In the past, most industrial health activity has been concerned with the physical effort needed for industrial output. Under cost pressure from Workmen's Compensation laws, companies have established safety departments responsible for guarding employees against physical injury, physical disability, and extreme physical fatigue. In many areas, standards have been established for how much physical exertion a worker can tolerate before performance deteriorates. Although limits for physical stress have been established, relatively little has been done formally (except in the Armed Forces) about establishing limits on the amount of mental stress that an individual can tolerate over prolonged periods.

With increased mechanization, more and more of the physical work in industry is being done by machines. Most business tasks require appreciably greater amounts of mental activity for their completion today than in the past. Yet only a very few of the most progressive companies have established programs designed to prevent mental fatigue and breakdown.[1] Perhaps one of the reasons for this is a widely held belief that our knowledge is still too meager to be very useful. We have far more confidence in our knowledge of what constitutes physical illness than we have in what we know about emotional or mental illness. In an age when over half the hospital beds in the United States are filled with mentally ill patients, the great disabler is not physical but mental and emotional disability.[2]

Standards for machine maintenance have long been in effect. We know that machinery periodically needs overhauling. A successful organization plans for this. But we do not know how long human beings can go without a rest, a raise, a training program, or some other form of appreciation from the organization before their performance begins to deteriorate or become counterproductive. We now know that people cannot live out their entire professional lives without regular overhauling of their knowledge and skills. As a result of rapidly changing technology, the half-life of an engineer is now said to be about 10 years. Perhaps accounting practices should treat human resources like capital assets, with percentage allowances for depreciation, overhaul, maintenance, and so on.

In their planning many companies today make provisions for their people. Managers in such companies recognize that the success of an organization depends to a major degree on the effective resolution of its human problems. In addition, judicial decisions in Workmen's Compensation have shown a growing tendency to find stressful employment responsible for damage to employees' mental health. Such decisions may soon force management to move further in establishing procedures for the proper care and maintenance of the mental health of its people.

Over the years there has been increasing awareness of the

importance of people to profits and, therefore, increasing concern with the more effective use of people. In earlier times, success came from the possession of machines or land; more recently, it might have been assured by the holding of key patents or industrial processes; but now the key to a corporation's continuing success is the innovative and executive ability of its staff.[3]

Much thought has been given to designing programs to increase personal effectiveness and express company concern for employees. The human relations program at the company where our study was made included extensive social and recreational aspects. Employee mass opinion surveys were conducted periodically, and at one time psychiatrist and psychologist consultants were hired on a part-time basis to help overcome employee difficulties by counseling on individual problems. As employees became more affluent, however, they were increasingly able to provide their own social and recreational activities.

It has been said that employee opinion surveys tend to uncover the "dissatisfiers" (those things that people complain about, the correction of which would not help them work more effectively) rather than the "demotivators" (those things that keep people from being more productive).[4] In addition opinion surveys have often resulted in additional recommendations and more work for managers already overburdened.

A more effective approach might be to offer employees opportunities and help in correcting the problems that personally concern them. Instead of hiring consultants on a part-time basis, it might be helpful to employ a full-time person who could personally experience the pressures and strains of the organization. A full-time person would be in a better position, because of greater familiarity with the organization, not only to help individuals with their difficulties, but to make recommendations to management for improving the work environment to prevent problems from recurring. Seeking solutions to its human problems may be the most crucial project a company can undertake, because, as Forrest H. Kirkpatrick put it:

> In a free economy, one company's only long-term advantage over another lies in its human resources. Advantages that arise from the opening of new markets, technological improvements,

lower materials or labor costs eventually prove to be relatively short run. This means that such qualities as initiative, drive, imagination, motivation and intelligence that are so much a part of what we call 'human resources' constitute the most important and meaningful substance that a company can count on for survival and growth.[5]

In the interests of the most effective development of these human resources, both for the fulfillment of the individual and the greater productivity of the organization, the conditions that inhibit employee creativity will be examined, with the hope that understanding will motivate change.

Notes

1.   Some of the more notable programs are those established at: the Metropolitan Life Insurance Co. in 1922; the R. H. Macy Co. in 1925; Western Electric's Hawthorne Plant in 1936; E. I. DuPont de Nemours and Co. in 1943; The Caterpillar Tractor Co. and The Hanes Hosiery Mills in 1945; Eastman Kodak Co. in 1946; American Cyanamid in 1947; Prudential Life Insurance Co. in 1948. In 1962, the Bureau of Business Research at the University of Texas sent out questionnaires to 1,000 companies selected because they were known to have relatively advanced personnel programs. Of 567 companies that replied, only 37 had formal mental health programs. (This figure does not include formal programs for helping alcoholics.) Only 10 of the 37 reported the use of either a full-time or part-time psychiatrist, and only 14 reported the use of a full-time or part-time psychologist. From: Charles A. Ferguson, *A Legacy of Neglect,* Industrial Mental Health Association, Fort Worth, 1965, pp. 16–24.

2.   Jack R. Ewalt, *Facts about Mental Illness,* National Association of Mental Health, Washington, D.C., 1961, p. 3.

3.   Gerald Piel, from *Consumers of Abundance,* Center for the Study of Democratic Institutions, Santa Barbara, Calif., June 1961.

4.   Frederick Herzberg, *Work and the Nature of Man* (Cleveland: World, 1966); and Herzberg, Mausner, and Schneiderman, *Motivation to Work* (New York: J. Wiley, 1959).

5.   Forrest H. Kirkpatrick, "Guidelines for Management Development," *The Personnel Administrator,* July–August 1963, p. 1.

two

The Organizational Climate

When we think of leadership, it is not uncommon to have in mind some type of highly personal, inspirational relationship between leader and followers. Leadership has its inspirational side, but emphasis upon this aspect tends to divert us from recognition of the actual skills required to elicit desired performance from a complex organization. The ultimate criterion of effective leadership must be, can only be, the quality of performance demonstrated by the organization's personnel, both individually and as a group. A leader has failed if he does not improve, or at least maintain the performance capabilities of the organization entrusted to him. Performance remains, of necessity, both the aim and the proof of his leadership. Leadership is the process of influencing individuals and organizations to obtain desired results.[1]

A major problem for those involved in the suicide process was that the managerial models they carried around in their heads did not correspond with the managerial model actually used in the organization. Because they were initially committed and interested in doing a good job, they would push to make things happen. Because they did not understand the rules of the game (and no one helped make the rules understandable), they made mistakes. After they had made enough mistakes and received subtle punishment for them, they began to feel that the game was not much fun. As a result, they pushed harder and harder until they were stepped on or they withdrew.

The four managerial stages through which organizations have progressed and are progressing could be compared to a triangle, an inverted triangle, a square, and a circle. *Pyramidal management*, represented by a triangle, is the management model that most managers carry around in their heads. In pyramidal management the boss sits at the top of the pyramid with middle managers in the middle and workers at the bottom. The boss at the top makes the decisions, which are relayed to the workers at the bottom for action. Not much happens until the boss makes a decision. The information flow is primarily from the top to the bottom.

The *inverted pyramidal management style,* represented by an inverted triangle, works differently. There is a slowly growing realization by management that the workers who are in contact with the problem often have the best answers. As the boss at the top has to deal with an organization that is growing increasingly complex, the pyramid is gradually reversed. The workers move to the top because they usually have the best solutions to organization problems and the quickest reaction time. Middle managers become a support to the workers, and top management functions as a support to the middle managers. The information flow is, as before, primarily from the top to the bottom, but because the pyramid is inverted, the flow is, in effect, reversed. The major problem with the inverted pyramid is that the whole organization rests on the point. This makes the organization unstable and puts a very heavy burden on the point. Bearing the weight of the entire organization, the boss begins to seek an alternative management style. The obvious solution is to broaden the base of the inverted pyramid to form a square.

Matrix management, represented by a square, was an effort to solve the problems of the inverted pyramidal management style. In addition to functional bosses along the sides of the square, project bosses were introduced along the top—which meant that each person in the organization suddenly had two bosses. A major rule in all organizations up to this point had been that each person in an organization should have only one boss. As Lincoln said, "A house divided against itself cannot stand." With matrix management, a person has two bosses, something new in the history of organizations. It requires a whole new set of skills, never before recognized as necessary, for a person to function with two bosses in an organization. It is not surprising that those committed to the organization had difficulty and began to engage in erratic behavior and to do things that others could not understand. But the situation gets worse!

"Circular management," represented by overlapping circles, was the next step in the evolution of management styles in typical American corporations. It originated in the aerospace industry, in which a wide variety of high technologies had to be integrated into solutions when it was obvious no one person had enough knowledge to make good decisions all alone. To put up a space capsule, decisions have to be made that require a knowledge of heat transfer, aerodynamics, materials, weight-to-thrust ratios, size, life-support systems, and so on. Because no one person could know enough to make such complicated decisions, a management style had to be evolved that would permit people to assume leadership when their areas of expertise were being discussed, to make inputs when other technologies affecting their areas of expertise were discussed and to develop ways of making the final decision a team rather than a one-person or a committee decision. As other organizations have developed increasingly sophisticated technologies, as marketing decisions have become increasingly complex, and as quality standards and product liability requirements have become increasingly severe, more and more organizations have had to move in this direction. Unfortunately this gradual shift in emphasis has rarely been made obvious to the members of the organizations. As a result a whole new profession called Organization Development has grown up to help organizations solve the kinds of problems precipitated by the increased complexities of business life.

Significant factors influencing worker attitude and behavior are the interpersonal and psychological climates within the organization. The most crucial aspect of the organizational climate is obviously the relationship between worker and boss. It will help to explain the organizational climate and its influence on the people in the company we studied if we trace the development of the company's managerial philosophy and its managerial attitude toward people. The author's experience in a wide variety of companies has shown that the evolution of management philosophy in this organization has not been atypical.

All organizations change with time. Before proceeding further, it is important to discuss the psychology of the work environment and some of the changes that have taken place over the years. These changes seem to divide rather naturally into four periods, with a management philosophy and an organizational climate characteristic of each. I have designated these periods (1) the scientific management era, (2) the human relations era, (3) management by subordinate commitment, and (4) management by team commitment. We have found that the management philosophies under discussion generally parallel those in other businesses and organizations during the past 40 years.

The Scientific Management Era

Following the Great Depression of 1929–1933 and up to the start of World War II, the predominate managerial style across the country was that of Taylor's Scientific Management.[2] The company in this study was a great deal smaller during that period, and engaged in the mass production of relatively simple-to-make parts. Because of this, relationships between people were more personal than contractual. Employees were predominately blue-collar workers, many from immigrant backgrounds. The tasks being performed were simple enough so that most of the relevant data could be held in a manager's head, with no need for large staffs and extensive reporting systems. Managers managed people in a typical hard-headed fashion as if they believed McGregor's Theory X assumptions:

1.   That people are inherently lazy, passive agents, needing to be manipulated and controlled by the organization, and that they must be motivated to work by management

2.   That people are primarily motivated by economic incentives and will do what gets them the greatest economic gain

3.   That organizations can and must be designed in such a way as to neutralize and control people's feelings and therefore their unpredictable traits

4.   That people's natural goals run counter to the organization's, that they are basically incapable of very much self-discipline and self-control, and that they must be controlled by external forces to ensure their working toward organizational goals

5.   That while most people fit the assumptions outlined above, there are a few who are self-motivated, self-controlled, less domi-

nated by their feelings; and this latter group (to which I have found most people *believe* they belong) must assume management responsibility for the others[3]

These paternalistic assumptions were not necessarily inappropriate in regard to the average worker of that period. Because the Depression (when many families did not have enough to eat) was still vivid in the minds of many workers, the average employee was primarily interested in meeting the physiological needs for food, clothing, and shelter.

The role of the manager during this period was essentially what Etzioni calls "calculative."[4] The organization bought the services of the employees for economic rewards and assumed the responsibility for directing and motivating the employees and itself through a rational system of rewards and controls. Certain job positions carried authority, and employees were expected to obey the persons holding these positions regardless of their personalities or experience. Organizational performance was management's responsibility. The organization established the limits of the employees' jobs, and the employees were expected to do no more than they were told to do. This seemed reasonable, considering the relative simplicity of the tasks and the lack of education of most employees.

Human Relations Management

With World War II came (1) the need for an expanded work force at the same time that men were entering the Armed Forces, with resulting labor shortages; (2) the increased employment of women; and (3) the allowability, under government contracts, of costs for obtaining people and keeping them satisfied. It became increasingly important to keep workers happy, and much of the cost of this could be borne by government cost-plus contracts. Workers also began to change. With the labor shortage, and because of the many other jobs available, they were more secure and less worried about losing the economic rewards of working. Recollections of the Depression began to recede, and workers began to look for jobs offering advantages other than just money.

It has been demonstrated that an increase in the size of a group decreases group cohesiveness and reduces member satisfaction. World War II expanded business rapidly just at the time when, because of labor shortages, workers could be more mobile. Therefore, ways had to be found to increase member satisfaction.

At about the same time, the Hawthorne Studies became widely known and encouraged changes in how managers dealt with their workers.[5] There were three findings from the Hawthorne Studies that caused particularly drastic alterations in management philosophy.[6] First, the experiments in the relay assembly test room demonstrated that the attention paid to workers by supervisors and the Harvard experts was more important for performance improvement than were the experimentally controlled changes in light, rest periods, and so on. Some social scientists and personnel managers took these findings to mean that the environment and the content of the job were unimportant and that the social climate between the supervisor and the subordinate was all that really counted.

Second, several thousand employees were interviewed about their attitudes and feelings regarding themselves, their coworkers, their supervisors, and the company. This program and its findings directed attention away from the jobs at which employees worked, and emphasized their inner psychological responses to the job environment as being most important.

Third, Roethlisberger and Dickson, the authors of the report, concluded that the factory had been set up and was being administered as though it cared only for the goals of the organization and little for the goals of the people involved. This approach frequently led to behavior (such as restricted output) that was not in the organization's best interest. For some behavioral scientists, these findings proved that the social work environment was more important than the physical work environment, and that the individual's goals were more important than the organization's goals in the development of efficient task accomplishment. The broad assumption that marked much of this research was that the human personality is unalterably opposed to formal organizations. People could, however, be motivated by placating them and giving rewards.

Throughout the forties and the fifties, the bulk of research by behavioral scientists in industry focused on the tendency of the formal organization to stunt and frustrate and make an apathetic nonentity of the individual worker. Although he has since modified his position considerably, Chris Argyris devoted an entire chapter in his book *Personality in Organization* to showing how incompatible were the needs of people with the demands of the organization.[7] Whyte's *The Organization Man* is another expression of the same point of view.[8]

As a result of the wartime business conditions and the influence of studies such as these, some companies, including the one in our study, developed "human relations programs." Extensive programs of social activities were launched—dinners, parties, buffets, golf outings, baseball leagues, bowling leagues, picnics, and free days at local amusement parks. Emphasis was placed on the company as "a good place to work." The approach was effective. People flocked to work and much of the cost of these programs was borne by cost-plus contracts.

These changes in the organizational environment resulted in a philosophy of management based on the assumptions that:

1.   People are basically motivated by social needs and obtain their basic sense of identity through relationships with others.

2.   As a result of the industrial revolution and the rationalization of work, meaning has gone out of work itself and must therefore be sought in social relationships on the job.

3.   People are more responsive to the social forces of the peer group than to the incentives and controls of management.

4.   People are responsive to management to the extent that supervisors can meet subordinates' social needs and needs for acceptance.[9]

During the human relations era, managers could no longer limit their concern solely to efficient task performance. They had to become concerned also with the social needs of their workers. More extensive personnel departments were developed whose primary duty was to maintain continuing surveillance of individual workers' morale. As workers' feelings became increasingly important, the managers' responsibilities began to shift from planning, organizing, motivating, and controlling to functioning as intermediaries between subordinates and higher management. The initiative for work began to shift from manager-organization responsibility to worker responsibility. Instead of being planners, organizers, and motivators of work, managers became the understanding expediters. In theory they still set goals, but they allowed greater latitude in the means by which subordinates would achieve those goals.

One explanation for the relative effectiveness of human relations management during this period was that workers had been trained in the Scientific Management philosophy. They expected to be dealt with in an authoritative Theory X way, and the human relations approach came as a welcome relief. For a time this provided a spurt of enthusiasm and a concomitant spurt in production.

Following World War II and the end of the Korean war came the temporary end of cost-plus contracts, a decrease in military manufacturing contracts, and an increase in the availability of hourly and salaried personnel. The return to civilian markets brought an increased emphasis on reducing costs and the need to become more competitive. The decline in cost-plus contracting meant that the cost of the human relations program had to come more and more from moneys which otherwise might have been added to profit.

During World War II the emphasis had been on the mass production of high-volume parts relatively easy to manufacture, but during the war years there had also been tremendous expansions in technology. With the decision to grow, the organization began to enter new markets requiring highly complex and complicated technology, which, in turn, required a different kind of worker. The ratio of white-collar workers to blue-collar workers changed drastically from 1 to 20 to, in one division, almost 1 to 1. The social-motivational approach of human relations management was less appropriate to the more sophisticated needs of the white-collar workers (scientists and Ph.D.'s), who were being hired in ever-increasing numbers. These people were more oriented to professional development and advancement than to the human relations approach of parties and sporting events.

There were corresponding stresses on management. It found itself attempting to manage a different kind of person; one who performed in an advanced, greatly diversified technology. Management had little training or familiarity with these fields. When making vacuum cleaners or valves, a manager could know almost all there was to know about the production process. But when building highly complex items, such as space power systems and rockets, many of which had never been built before, many of the most critical decisions had to be placed in the hands of subordinate technical experts. No longer were things being made that could be encompassed within the scope of one mind. No longer could an all-knowing person at the top decide on the goals and the functional responsibilities for people engaged in the manufacture of such highly sophisticated items.

As a result of various pressures from the external environment, increased competition, advanced technology, a different type of worker unmotivated by techniques useful before, and new and different work to be done, a new managerial philosophy evolved to handle these complex forces within the organization. This philosophy has been called by various names, including: management by exception, management by default, management by individual commitment, existential management, and management by subordinate commitment—the term we shall use.

Management by Subordinate Commitment

Warren Bennis describes it as "organization by inkblot," ". . . an actor steals around an uncharted wasteland growing more restive and paranoid by the hour while he waits for orders that never come."[10] Under this managerial style the only goals, other than very broad ones such as "growth" or "maximizing profit," are those of individuals or of coalition subgroups. Whatever organizational goals may have existed are kept hidden because, as one manager stated, "If the people know what the organizational goals are, they will only work against them." The manager's job is basically to wend one's way through the pressures from various individuals and subgroups while attempting to please as many people and offend as few as possible.

Following are some of the implicit assumptions associated with management by subordinate commitment:

1.   People are interested only in their personal goals. They are not basically interested in meeting organizational objectives, and it is best not to discuss organizational objectives with them because they will only work against you.

2.   The best way to run an organization is to hire aggressive people and then respond to as many of the pressures from them as you can. The world is changing so fast and the pressures on management are so varied and complex that there cannot be any organizational objectives anyway.

3.   The best way to motivate people is to offer them opportunities for confronting challenges and for self-actualization. (However, if the challenges are too big or come too quickly, while providing only minimal rewards, then the "suicides" begin to occur. As one person said, "It begins to seem that confronting challenges successfully only gets me more challenges to confront.")

4.   Authority is rarely delegated because this would place some responsibility for errors on the person doing the delegating. Instead, people are left "free" to do anything as long as it is the "right" thing.

5.   Responsibility is not assigned, but it should be assumed (seized) eagerly by committed people. People are evaluated on the measure of their commitment. (This term is so vague that it leaves much room for individual and unsubstantiated interpretation, adding to the general climate of anxiety and resulting in people working longer and longer hours as a means of proving commitment.)

6.   Titles and organizational prerogatives are unimportant to committed people. (This reduces the pressure on management to determine who gets these limited rewards, as well as reducing the need to reach decisions about whose contributions are most worthwhile.)

Management seeks eagerly for charismatic leaders who can inspire others to do the necessary jobs without making organizational demands. They want subordinates who will change defeatist attitudes into positive "can do" attitudes (and because they believe that good leaders are born, not trained, they see little need for leadership development programs).

Because management by subordinate commitment is destructive to bright, aggressive, committed individuals within the organization, this philosophy is eventually damaging to the organization itself. Bright young people who might develop into inspirational leaders are given increasingly difficult tasks to perform until they eventually find one they cannot handle alone. When this happens, a reevaluation takes place and the organization comes to the conclusion that competency was not there after all.

Because people are expected to work individually and unofficially (one might even say surreptitiously) on tasks, they are usually unable to significantly alter the course of a large organization except at great cost to themselves. Martyrdom and suicide are frequently the ultimate result. Without direction from knowledgeable leaders, the organization has to run on subordinate enthusiasm, which is rarely equal to the task for any extended period.

The psychological contract is one in which the worker is expected to be wholeheartedly committed to the accomplishment of an organizational goal which has personal significance for the worker. This goal is often not made explicit to others in the organization, with whom the individual must frequently compete for time and scarce materials. Noncommitted people can back off, but committed people (like the Kamikaze pilots of World War II) keep on fighting against great odds until something—frequently self-destructive—finally happens.

Managing by subordinate commitment is essentially an opportunistic approach to managing, in which subordinates are expected to be committed while management remains largely uncommitted. Because there are so many unknowns (or because management is so overwhelmed by what it does not know), there can be no real plans. A philosophy is accepted that one has to manage day to day, crisis by crisis. The key to survival is to "stay loose" and be opportunistic when opportunities occur. Everything becomes guesswork, and not guessing at all is often better than a poor guess for which one might be held accountable. As a result, decisions are delayed until forced by circumstances—usually a crisis of one kind or another. Decisions made under the stress of crisis are seldom very creative, however.

There are certain advantages to *management by subordinate commitment,* for example, when highly trained workers are performing complex, rapidly changing tasks for a traditional management largely uneducated about these tasks. The advantages, however, may be outweighed by negative side effects, such as confusion about goals and their priorities, individual competitiveness, lack of trust and cooperative effort, and the loss of good people which this style of management seems to cause.

Management by Team Commitment

An alternative style to management by subordinate commitment is one that might be called "management by team commitment." Under management by team commitment, all-inclusive goals are defined (first between the subordinate and the boss and then, most importantly, with the team). As a result, the team concentrates on common rather than individual accomplishments. With the overall goals defined, the individual has a way of determining which of various alternatives is most likely to be appreciated and rewarded by the organization, and thus can choose to channel efforts toward organizational rather than purely personal goals. A basis for trust and cooperation is established because those working in similar areas have something in common. Because one another's goals are known, assistance can be offered and received on some basis other than purely personal advantage.

The fundamental assumptions about people made under a philosophy of management by team commitment are that:

1. Most employees want to work and to contribute to some purpose or goal larger than themselves.

2. Each individual is unique and management must be individualized; that is, no standardized managerial style will work for everyone.

3. Individuals are sufficiently flexible to mesh individual goals with team goals if the team knows what these goals are.

4. To coordinate the efforts of many people (and release energy): first, there must be *meaningful* communication among group members; second, superordinate goals must be determined so that team energy can be constructively channeled; third, a new kind of leadership is required and new skills must be learned.

People under pressure (and most people in business today are under pressure) cannot cooperate for very long solely on their own initiative. They need help from a leader to decide on a common purpose and a common plan for achieving this. In informal groups a leader will usually evolve from the group to fulfill this function. In business groups with a leadership vacuum, the evolution of a leader from the group poses a threat (real or imagined) to the designated leader. Trust and cooperation are not fostered in leaderless, purposeless groups, but come from working together in a common effort toward a common goal in which both the group and its individual members are interested.

The problems in other management styles were either: too much emphasis on organization goals (scientific management), too little emphasis on organization goals (human relations management), or too much emphasis on individual goals (management by subordinate commitment). Leaderless, purposeless groups do not accomplish worthwhile results except through tremendous sacrifices (suicides) by individual members. There are just too many people to fight in a large organization. In an organization where resources are in short supply, the predatory, "self-actualizing" persons who are able to take from others what they need are likely to survive; while the humanitarian, self-sacrificing individuals, unable to meet all the needs of such a large group, find themselves becoming more and more drained and may eventually end up as suicides. Leadership in the future will not be leadership by default or leadership with only the subordinates committed, but rather leadership characterized by group goal setting, team building, and the meeting of subordinates' needs on an individualized basis. As people and their tasks change, the psychological climate and the managerial tone of the organization will also change. This evolution should be in a direction that encourages the retention of good people and the efficient, effective accomplishment of the necessary tasks. Table 2-1 shows the

Table 2-1 Evolution of Managerial Style in a Typical Company

Managerial Style	Scientific Management	Human Relations Management	Management by Subordinate Commitment	Management by Team Commitment
When Most Prevalent	Prior to World War II	World War II to end of Korean war and end of cost-plus contracting	End of Korean war to present	The future
Tasks	Simple	Simple	Complex, requiring *low* degree of group interaction	Complex, requiring *high* degree of group interaction
Business Environment	Stable with minor risks	Changing but little competition	Rapidly changing with increasing competition	Rapidly changing, highly complex, with increasing risks
Type of Contracts	Firm, fixed price	Cost plus fixed fee	Cost plus incentive fee	Fixed price
Dominant Roles	The industrial engineer (task simplification)	The personnel man and the party giver	The P.R. man and the scientist working alone	The planner, the team builder and the systems engineer
Motivating Force	Pressure from management	Subordinate gratitude for social needs being met	Youthful subordinates' high commitment to personal tasks	Group commitment to group tasks
Psychological Environment	Hard work but resentment under management pressure	Social atmosphere	Frenzy, anxiety, confusion	Hard-work under internalized and peer-group pressure
Philosophical Base	Calvinism (the purpose of life is hard work)	Freudian child psychology (frustration avoidance) and Christian Science (mental manipulations can overcome all obstacles)	Existential psychology (existence purposeless except as individually defined here and now)	Ego psychology (development of reality orientation to environment) and group psychology (definition of what is needed to accomplish group purposes)

Followers: Technically	Unskilled	Skilled	Skilled & professional	Skilled & professional
Psychologically	Want material needs met	Want social needs met	Want opportunities to perform and prove selves, i.e., recognition	Want opportunities for service and sense of accomplishment
Expectations of Subordinates	Obedience and hard work	Happiness	Total commitment and ability to correct problems with minimal or no organizational assistance	Solve problems with organizational help
Leaders: Technically	Knowledgeable	Knowledgeable	Not knowledgeable	Knowledgeable
Psychologically	Authoritative Make all decisions Retain authority	Appeasing Calculative	Defensive Make few decisions Retain authority Responsibility up for grabs	Open Help group make decisions Share authority Share responsibility
Management's Responsibility	Plan Organize	Maintain friendly relationships and keep people happy	Provide challenge, then stay out of way so people can work. See that people have tasks but fewer organizational resources than needed. Pass on some information.	Help group to set goals. Facilitate group process. Accept responsibility for effective group functioning. Integrate subordinates' goals with organizational objectives.

Table 2-1 Evolution of Managerial Style in a Typical Company *(Continued)*

Managerial Style	Scientific Management	Human Relations Management	Management by Subordinate Commitment	Management by Team Commitment
Advantages	Management by simple formulas possible	Workers happier, but only as long as appeased.	Conflict can be ignored Managers can manage without technical knowledge Many people can work with minimal technical direction, but may not be oriented toward group goals	Group oriented toward organizational, not just personal, goals Possibility for many people to make goal-oriented contribution to business
Disadvantages	Only manager has much impact on goals or managing business. Resentment generated in workers Anti-organization subgroups form.	Reduction of efforts toward organization's goals	People frequently work at cross purposes Absence of group goals leaves little opportunity for recognition except by satisfying individual needs, which may not be organizationally relevant Commitment cannot be quickly turned off, but sometimes goes on after usefulness ends Suicide of useful people	Managers must develop skill in: goal setting group dynamics conflict resolution confrontation versatility interpersonal competence
Typical Management Grid Styles[11]	9.1 Managers produce 1.1 subordinates	1.9	1.1 Managers expect 9.9 subordinates	9.9 Managers develop 9.9 subordinates

evolution of managerial styles in typical U.S. corporations and the various factors responsible for each new stage.

The morale of an organization and the results that it gets from its employees are the products of management behavior over a number of years. They are the products of the total management process. It is not possible to conjure up favorable employee attitudes in a time of crisis after years of relative neglect. Employee attitudes at any particular time are an accumulation of the net impressions on the individual of all that management *is doing* and *has been doing* over an extended period, not what management *says* it is doing or has been doing.

Employee attitudes and organizational morale are a result of the way employees are introduced into the organization, the kind of work they are given to do, the way they are supervised and compensated, and the way they are advanced on the job. They are also affected by the way organizational changes are made, the way layoffs occur, and the reputation of the management for honest information and good faith.

Management's behavior is under constant scrutiny and is continually being evaluated by the employees as well as by stockholders and the financial community. Obviously, the task of pleasing everyone is not easy. In the past, too little reliable information has been available, and what has been available has been the product of hearsay, the wishful thinking of personnel men and supervisors, or the questionable results of opinion polls.

A major task facing management is to make a realistic reexamination of its management policies and programs and to reevaluate and reshape present performance and long-range goals in the light of a changing environment and rapidly changing needs. Tradition is not enough, and good intentions are not enough. An organization will be as inefficient as its management will tolerate; inefficiency will be prevented in direct proportion to management interest.

> If management is concerned over lack of motivation and goal directed behavior among employees, it must look to itself for the reasons and it must treat itself if it is to effect a cure.[12]

Notes

1. Joseph A. Olmstead, "The Skills of Leadership," *Military Review,* March 1967, pp. 62–70.

2. Frederick Winslow Taylor, *Scientific Management* (New York: Harpers, 1911).

3. Douglas McGregor, *The Human Side of Enterprise* (New York: McGraw-Hill, 1960).

4. Amatai Etzioni, *Modern Organizations* (Englewood Cliffs, N.J.: Prentice-Hall, 1964).

5. Elton Mayo, *The Social Problems of an Industrial Civilization* (Boston: Harvard Business School, 1945).

6. Peter B. Zaill, "Industrial Engineering and Socio-Technical Systems," *The Journal of Industrial Engineering,* vol. XVIII, no. 9, Sept. 1957, pp. 530–538.

7. Chris Argyris, *Personality in Organization* (New York: Harper and Row, 1957), chap. 3.

8. William H. Whyte, Jr., *The Organization Man* (Garden City, N.Y.: Doubleday, 1957).

9. Edgar H. Schein, *Organizational Psychology* (Englewood Cliffs, N.J.: Prentice-Hall, 1965), p. 51.

10. Warren G. Bennis, "The Coming Death of Bureaucracy," *Think,* Nov.–Dec. 1966, p. 30.

11. Robert Blake and Jane Mouton, *The Managerial Grid* (Houston: Gulf, 1964).

12. Charles Hughes, *Goal Setting* (New York: American Management Association, 1965), p. 56.

three

The Suicide Process

Company executives are the most emotionally
exploited, loneliest, unhappy, unrepresented and
misunderstood group of workers in our society.[1]

We cannot expect everyone to go on "taking
it" while exhorting them to make a "good
social adjustment" to obviously demoralizing
circumstances and treatment.[2]

The foundation for later suicide is laid when an individual first
joins the organization, accepts a vague, nonpublic charter, and
enters a system where the goals (and thus success in reaching
them) are poorly defined and where the philosophy is one of
managing by subordinate commitment. On entering the organization, the new employee accepts this in good faith, but as time
passes disillusionment grows, and the problems of unfulfilled
needs become greater and greater. The disparity between expectation and reality is upsetting, and produces severe internal stress.
The end result is some action, either precipitous or gradual,
which we have here called professional suicide.

Suicide is also a result of the psychological reactions to overcommitment. When people care very deeply about something it
becomes too important when things do not go right.

The process of professional suicide can be divided into seven
merging and overlapping stages: (1) acceptance of a vague
charter, (2) the honeymoon period, (3) testing of the charter and
of organizational backing, (4) conflict within the employee over
the charter, (5) the search for support or resolution from the boss

(the formal system), (6) the search for support from peers (the informal system), and (7) symptom formation. Each of these stages will be discussed in greater detail.

Acceptance of a Vague Charter

The process of professional suicide frequently begins when an individual is first hired and is provided with only a vague charter of what is expected. It is not uncommon in organizations with high professional suicide rates for a new employee to be given a charter without formal organizational backing. Under a philosophy of management by subordinate commitment, a great effort is made to hire "capable" people who, with only vague charters and minimal feedback, can solve problems and help reach organizational goals. The boss approaches the employee on a personal rather than an organizational basis because of the boss's own (1) lack of commitment or (2) inability to commit the organization to what the boss wants done or (3) fear of upsetting others because the new employee's charter overlaps with what someone else is already doing.

The complexities of modern business make it difficult to specify precisely everything that the new employee will do, but this is not the issue here. Charters are frequently left purposely vague, because the boss is unable or unwilling to think through more fully just what should really be done, as greater specification would require. Also nonvague charters would require greater clarification about the overlap between the new person's charter and existing charters. Bosses are frequently unwilling to clarify who does what, preferring that subordinates "fight it out" on their own. In the process of fighting it out someone frequently gets hurt. (Tables 3-1 and 3-2 present some of the advantages and disadvantages of unclear charters from management's and subordinates' points of view.)

The new employee cannot always easily ascertain the lack of formal organizational support. The boss's charge is accepted in good faith, but the lack of organizational support makes itself insidiously felt by such questions from peers as "Who says so?" or "What does your boss's boss think?" The degree of real orga-

Table 3-1 Advantages and Disadvantages of Unclear Charters from *Management's* Point of View

Advantages	Disadvantages
Saves time (in the short run).	Costs time (in the long run).
Saves energy (in the short run).	Costs energy (in the long run).
Saves emotional stress (in the short run).	Costs emotional stress (in the long run).
No need to spend time clarifying knotty issues.	Issues not clarified as fully as possible in the beginning have a way of getting worse.
No need to confront (in the short run) organizational issues of overlapping charters and who does what.	The issue of overlapping charters and who does what gets harder to solve over time except as the result of suicides.
Lots of people responsible for everything. (Someone will do it.)	When lots of people are responsible for everything, nothing gets done. Responsibilities fall through the gaps when overlap becomes too intense.
Because the problem is one of "interpretation," management is less likely to be held responsible.	Peers are upset when someone takes initiative in working on a management problem. It can be taken to mean that the boss's work is not good enough if someone else has to start helping.

nizational support is also measured by how much authority and how many resources are actually delegated to the individual. In any organization there are many demands on each member. The more experienced members become skillful in determining which activities have a potential payoff for them (will win them something from the organization), and whose needs and which activities are relatively unimportant (will not win them anything).

The psychological contract is the sum total of these expectations, written and unwritten, spoken and unspoken, between the employees and the employer. These expectations are not completely discussed at the time of employment or subsequently, because there are fond, unstated hopes which might be dashed if discussed too explicity or because each has implicit (but conflict-

Table 3-2   Advantages and Disadvantages of Unclear Charters from *Subordinates'* Points of View

Advantages	Disadvantages
If I am adroit (capable), I may be able to develop this job into a bigger one than originally intended.	If I am not adroit (capable) enough, I may be cut down by others with vague charters and not be allowed by the system to accomplish much.
I can wheel and deal and do what I want.	The wheeling and dealing of others creates confusion for me and makes me less effective.
If I keep the situation as vague as possible, perhaps the unspecified will be defined to my advantage.	I become anxious because I do not know what my job really is or on what results I will be judged.
	The lack of clear and public charters makes others wonder what I am doing. It creates anxiety, suspicion and hostility about me and my role in the organization.
	If my vague charter is not constantly defended, my responsibilities can be taken over by someone else. As a result, I am reluctant to accept help or let anyone learn too much about my job.

ing) assumptions that seem too obvious to discuss. The expectations change with time and with contact with others in the organization. As a result, the individual's status and role in the organization may become quite unclear after a relatively brief time because of the constantly changing environment. A major cause of professional suicide is actual or perceived changes in the nature of the psychological contract between the employee and the employer. The frustrated efforts of an employee to clarify a vague charter with a boss who has difficulty in being open frequently signal the employee's entrance into the suicide process.

People involved in professional suicide seem to be the young, dynamic, idealistic ones, with whom it is possible for aging bosses to identify.[3] To encourage these young people to work hard, promises are held out which may not be entirely realistic, for example, "Work hard and you can be president of the company." The more practical, more experienced, older employees rarely allow themselves to be drawn into such compacts.

In addition to having unclear charters, newcomers must compete for a portion of their tasks with old-timers, who have developed relationships throughout the organization and know many informal ways of making life easy for themselves and difficult for new employees. The length of time individuals can live with vague, nonpublic charters is directly related to their levels of personal competence, and to the extent to which they can act in ways nonthreatening to the formal organization while going about duties the organization does not fully accept or understand.

The lack of clarity in organizational goals is a very real problem closely related to unclear charters. Although people in most sections of the organization would claim to be interested in organizational growth and profits, many of their actions seem more geared to perpetuating a particular power structure and the status quo.

The Honeymoon Period

Following the employee's acceptance of a vague charter, there is usually a brief time that might be called "the honeymoon period." Because of the lack of structure and clearly defined roles, every new employee is viewed apprehensively as a potential competitor, but every new employee is also viewed as a source of help. Because people are not sure if the new employee will help or hurt, they are initially quite helpful. Since they are unsure of how much power the newcomer really has, they cooperate.

During the honeymoon period everyone appears so friendly that the individual may be fooled into too much self-revelation, which may then be placed on the grapevine and later used against the new employee.

Testing the Charter

Sooner or later people find out that the new employee is no superman and cannot solve all the problems in the organization alone. Then there is usually some testing of how much power the individual really has, and perhaps some withdrawing because the individual has not been as helpful as was fantasied. During this phase there is testing of how much of the vague charter will be supported by the organization and how much of it will have to be effected on a personal, informal basis. This usually centers around testing by both the organization and the individual to see what resources will be made available to do the job. Vital resources may be either allocated or withheld. These can be classified as material resources, people resources, and authority. Material resources include such things as office space, telephone lines, and various kinds of equipment. People resources include the time of people, which may be either officially or unofficially granted. Authority is the right to "sign off on" (approve or disapprove) certain organizational actions. An additional resource is certain symbols of organizational prestige, which may be granted or withheld, such as private parking spaces and keys to the building. While these do not, in themselves, provide authority, they establish a certain kind of organizational status (no matter how much this may be formally denied) and thus help to obtain cooperation.

It is during the testing stage that organizational disillusionment begins. Few managers realize the extent to which workers get information, not from the written or the spoken word but, rather, from their own experience and the experience of others: "Too often it appears that on this job, at least, when I give my employer what he says he wants, it appears to have mighty little to do with my getting what I want."

Conflict within the Employee

Psychological strength comes from being included, trusted, and respected. In an individually competitive environment, where the management style is one of subordinate commitment, this strength is hard to find because there is a short-term competitive advantage for long-term employees in not including, respecting, or trusting new employees. During this stage, people frequently experience what has been called culture shock. The new employees find they do not understand the organization, cannot communicate in meaningful ways with it, are not respected (respect is earned through communicating), and are not regarded as competent because they cannot communicate.

When people are forced to deal with ambiguous situations, they become increasingly anxious and apprehensive. Like someone lost in a jungle not knowing from which direction the next attack will come, they may react by running in panic, shooting wildly until their ammunition is exhausted, plodding onward with vacant eyes, or sitting immobilized waiting for fate to overtake them. All are negatively affected in that they lose spontaneity and self-confidence. Specific *behavior* is related to the individual's own personality, but the *problem* is that of being lost. What is needed is a purpose, a direction, and a plan, which would help focus on a solution and give the employees some sense of mastery over their destiny.

Obviously, some will set personal goals and, drawing a set of friends around them, proceed toward these goals. But most, I believe, would prefer working toward organizational goals if such goals could be established and were supported.

The Search for Resolution from the Boss (the Formal System)

The individual's frustration grows with the gradual realization of having accepted a commitment for a project that has not been officially sanctioned and the difficulties that ensue; such as peer-group hostility over feared charter infringement, the fostering of individual competitiveness and the resulting lack of trust, the communication problems and lack of knowledge about what is going on, and the anxiety and time pressures which make it hard to establish strong peer-group relationships. The individual gradually becomes aware that some of these difficulties result from organizational and top management inadequacies. Efforts to confront the boss with these problems often cause the boss to feel guilty and defensive and to begin avoiding a subordinate who generates such feelings. A subordinate who can maintain frequent personal contacts with the boss feels some support. However, as other demands become more pressing, and as the subordinate applies more pressure for clarification, the boss may become more and more defensive and resolve the situation by finding less and less time to give the subordinate.

What is needed is an official notice to the organization of the individual's charter and the responsibilities contained in it. However, the problem that made the charter vague in the first place keeps it from being clarified. Without clarification, problems continue to develop, the promised satisfactions do not come, the chaos is not alleviated; but instead, with more pressure, grows gradually worse. The individual slowly comes to realize that the situation is not what it originally appeared to be. The organization's half-hearted help and the various objections raised by peers make the boss feel that undertaking to clarify the charter would not be politically advisable at this time. The boss assumes that if the subordinate were competent enough, there would be no need to clarify the charter. And, thus, pressure for charter clarification further alienates the subordinate from the boss. Any efforts to clarify the charter with the boss's boss are obviously seen as a threat and would further compromise the subordinate.

The Search for Support from Peers (the Informal System)

In addition to trying to reach some resolution with the boss, the individual also tries to resolve the situation with peers. A major problem here is the competitive struggle among peers. In management by subordinate commitment, everyone beside—or above—oneself is potentially a rival. Theoretically, one can advance by doing a good job, but in an organization where only the present crises count and the remembrance of good jobs done in the past is short-lived, old-timers have noticed that advancement can often be achieved more quickly by easing out the competition than by doing a good job themselves. So they spend much organizational time getting to know their rivals' problems and circulating them to those persons' disadvantage. Rivals can be rendered unimportant and ineffectual through the subtle use of gossip and noncooperation. It is important to do this carefully so that no word gets back to incite countermeasures.

When people are not clear about what they should be doing, they frequently become anxious upon learning of the good work of others. The more competent a newcomer appears, the more there is to fear. With vague charters, there are large swings in the organization's activities, depending on what seems important to the boss at the moment. Gradually the newcomer learns that if you tell persons in your area what you are doing, the anxiety generated by their knowing what you do (while unclear about their own responsibilities) tends to make them say either, "It is not important enough for you to do; you should not be doing that," or "I should be doing that." As a result, peers seem to advocate removing all activity from the newcomer's jurisdiction.

In complex organizational life with only vague charters, employees cannot rely solely on their boss for evaluations of their effectiveness or the usefulness of their activities. They must engage in continuing dialogue with people throughout the organization in order to find out what truly is most useful. To be successful, it is important to maintain good peer relationships; but, unfortunately, peer goals and values frequently run counter to formal organization goals and values.

Symptom Formation

The individual who discovers the impossibility of fulfilling the commitment made to a supposedly sympathetic boss becomes increasingly frustrated and angry. The mounting frustration and aggressiveness (which usually cannot be explained to authority figures without increased defensiveness on the boss's part) gradually become more and more pervasive if not resolved. Attempts to resolve the situation with peers (whom one hopes will understand) may be unsuccessful and only result in further alienating them. If the problem continues without correction, the individual will first become angry and isolated, then depressed and isolated. Without a sympathetic listener, attempts to break out of the pattern may result in further defeat, loss of self-respect, and isolation. As the process continues, the individual becomes more and more trapped by personal commitments to a task that, it is now realized, never had full organizational support; and eventually begins trading on personal relationships in order to accomplish the assigned tasks. Because of lack of organizational backing, the employee may finally run out of personal relationships and at the same time find himself in open competition with the formal organization. It is then that most leave the organization or withdraw into relative inactivity.

Individuals whose commitments are great enough and whose hopes for their projects are dashed suddenly will have fairly violent reactions against the authority figures and the organization which, it is felt, have betrayed them. Attempts to discuss this anger and frustration will be perceived as an attack, which it is. The authority figure whose insecurity is partly responsible for the original deception will feel threatened by this and will fight back by disclaiming any responsibility. This, of course, intensifies the individual's feelings of injustice, frustration, and anger, and adds to the feeling of abandonment. Furthermore, the individual now becomes a constant reminder of the boss's own inability to support the job, which, in turn, arouses the boss's guilt and anger, and inspires the conscious or unconscious wish to remove the source of irritation as quickly as possible.

Caught in the vortex of these emotions, the individual becomes like a person dangling at the end of a rope, aware that struggling may only serve to tighten the noose. The choice is to die quietly or to struggle to get free, unaided by those who observe the struggles as they rationalize that the individual chose to be in this predicament. And perhaps, in some measure, this is so; if the employee had not become committed to an organizational task for which there was inadequate support, this situation might not have come about.

Vague fears cause the individual to close up and become less accessible, depriving himself of the relationships and the communications needed to be successful in accomplishing tasks. Confidence is weakened; barriers develop, causing gradual separation from others and from support needed to stay healthy and grow professionally.

An organization *needs* cooperative environments. They foster involvement; and a growing person *needs* to be involved. A person who is a part of something has a reason to become responsible. Most people want to see something worthwhile evolve from their efforts, and will often work in spite of organizational prohibitions. Some of these efforts (especially those which can be carried on in isolation, such as inventing) are eventually rewarded, while others bring only increasing amounts of organizational hostility. Sacrificing one's time and effort is worthy and may gain management's praise; however, by sacrificing too much, one may become unavailable to the organization. A key factor in professional suicide is that some people commit too much of themselves to organizations which provide too few safeguards (and do not seem to care).

Failure to live up to boss and organizational expectations is often regarded as willful misbehavior, not only by bosses and the organization, but by individuals as well. Lack of success (even in performing nearly impossible tasks) is followed by a strong guilt reaction and a consequent desire for self-punishment, which the organization does little to prevent. When the culture (either national or organizational) regards suicide (in the physical sense) as an honorable and noble way to solve a problem, suicides tend to occur more frequently. The suicide rate is much higher in Asia than in the United States or England, and "professional suicide" is much more prevalent in some companies than in others.

Potential suicides are easily distinguished, in the final phases at least, from the anxiety-ridden or the overtly depressed, in that they exhibit little anxiety or depression about their state. Suicide seems to hold more appeal for them than does continuation of an unsatisfying existence. Professional suicide is seen as an appropriate resolution for an impossible dilemma. To be acceptable, professional suicide must fulfill four conditions: reduction of conflicts, compatibility with ego-ideals, continuing of personal relationships, and fulfillment of fantasies.

When frustrating experiences are carried out with kindness and consideration, there is no legitimate way to express anger and frustration, and guilt can then become intense. It appears that the guilt and loss of self-respect that come with not seeing oneself as doing a good enough job keep some people in an organization long after they might otherwise have left.

Even a new-born baby can feel the difference between being treated with respect or as a nonentity. The feeling of not being respected or wanted starts the closing-off process, which leads to becoming more and more cut off from others, and, if completed, results in suicide. Kobler and Stotland found that suicide is often the outcome of a series of unsatisfying social interactions.[4] Professional suicide, like physical suicide, occurs in those who feel rejected and that their psychological and physical resources have been exhausted. Loneliness is a frequent factor in both professional and physical suicide.[5]

Suicidal crisis may be best understood as the last stages in the progressive breakdown of adaptational behavior in emotionally exhausted people. The early symptoms of potential suicide include talking about the subject, self-injury and self-neglect, and depression and panic.

A therapist who recognizes a suicidal crisis should candidly explore the person's feelings of despair.[6] The antidote for these feelings is increased management support, rather than seeing the employee as an irretrievable failure.

Guidelines for therapy for potential physical suicides call for maintaining contact with the patients and reestablishing their communication with the rest of the world. Patients need help in reconstituting their sense of identity. They benefit from emergency psychological support and stimulation toward constructive action.[7] Free communication is most important. Family, friends, and community agencies should be mobilized to aid the patient. Individuals intent on killing themselves still wish to be rescued or to have their deaths prevented. Suicide prevention requires recognizing that the individual is in some state of equilibrium between wishing to live and wishing to die.[8]

Notes

1.   William F. Miller, "Expert Finds Executives Inept at Job Hunting," *The Plain Dealer,* Sept. 2, 1968, p. 1-B.

2.   Lawrence K. Frank, "The Promotion of Mental Health," *Mental Health in*

the United States, The Annals of the American Academy of Political and Social Sciences, vol. 286, March 1963, p. 169.

3. As used here, "young" does not necessarily refer to chronological age but to a dynamic, positive attitude toward change and a willingness to consider alternative points of view.

4. Arthur L. Kobler and Ezra Stotland, *The End of Hope, A Social-Clinical Study of Suicide* (Glencoe, Ill.: Free Press, 1964).

5. Peter Sainsbury, *Suicides in London: An Ecological Study* (London: Chapman and Hall, 1955).

6. Chad Varah (ed.), *The Samaritans* (New York: McMillan, 1965).

7. Robert E. Litman, "Emergency Response to Potential Suicide," *Journal of Michigan State Medical Society,* 62; pp. 68–72, January 1963.

8. Hans Selye, *The Stress of Life* (New York: McGraw-Hill, 1956).

four

Individual Characteristics Contributing to the Suicide Process

. . . the individual in our society who does have an aggressive problem-solving orientation is often considered ill-mannered. And as everyone knows, it is much easier to bear the stigma of immorality than of bad manners! The problem solver is unquestionably a deviant, and making good use of him is one of the major challenges of our society. A revealing experiment on this has been devised by Shepard. He gave a problem to a series of groups created for the purpose of the experiment. Some of these groups contained a "deviant," others did not. In every case, the group containing a deviant came out with a richer analysis of the problem and a more elegant solution. The next step was to request each group to throw out one member. The deviant was thrown out every time! As long as the group had to work with him, the results were creative, but faced with the choice, the group found it easier to continue minus the person who forced them to confront conflicting views and integrate them[1]

There are a number of personality characteristics that contribute to individuals becoming enmeshed in the process of professional suicide. Chief among these is a self-sacrificing, humanitarian approach to life, which urges them to become involved and committed to situations in which they are less concerned with self-protection than with making a contribution. Management by subordinate commitment encourages an individual to commit himself to the organization, but the organization remains largely uncommitted to the individual.

The end result of management by subordinate commitment is the generation of a great deal of frustration for the subordinate. He is expected to do his own goal setting, his own planning, his own coordination, his own information gathering, obtain cooperation on his own, and to do all this with minimal authority by trading on his own personal appeal. He is expected to assume more and more responsibility, and to subsist with extremely limited organizational resources. He is expected to remain optimistic and energetic.

Our study found that professional suicide is the result of an interaction between certain characteristics in the individual and certain characteristics in the organizational environment. We will first discuss individual characteristics which contribute to the suicide process. These can be divided into two broad categories: (1) normal characteristics or needs which, if not met, cause people severe difficulty and perhaps even eventual suicide and (2) certain basically self-destructive characteristics within the individual (usually a result of severe frustration) which provoke or hasten the suicide process.

There are certain basic needs common to almost all human beings. An organization that does not recognize and make provisions for meeting these needs will probably have many people leaving it or becoming disruptive within it as they become frustrated in their attempts to get their needs met. Environments that make meeting these needs difficult can be called stressful. People who cannot arrange to get their needs met, because of characteristics within either the organizational environment or themselves, are people under stress.

The common human needs, according to Maslow, are:

1. The need for food, clothing and shelter
2. The need for a sense of security
3. The need to belong

4.   The need for recognition and a sense of self-esteem

5.   The need to grow and develop (to self-actualize)[2]

In addition to the five human needs described by Maslow, there are two others included by Erik Fromm in his list of basic human needs, but not generally recognized by Existentialists (or by those whose management philosophy is subordinate commitment). These are:

6.   The need for a sense of purpose

7.   The need for a structure from which to view the world.[3]

People need food, clothing and shelter. Organizations must meet these needs or people would have to work elsewhere. It is the need for food, clothing, and shelter that first brought people into groups and caused them to work together. In the modern welfare state, however, few people starve to death. Some means of motivating people to work more effective than food, clothing and shelter must be found, because in an affluent society these things can be obtained without working. Few organizations would attempt to obtain workers without a plan for meeting these well-recognized needs, but they may not accept or even recognize some of the other needs.

People need a sense of security, which in our society is usually provided for by unions or the social welfare system or company benefits, and usually outside the work process. This need seems to be met without regard to how ineffectively or creatively a person works and is therefore little motivation to do good work.

People need to belong somewhere, and the most important sense of belonging comes from a person's job. One may belong to a family, a church, a lodge, or a golf club, but most important is usually the job—especially for professionals and especially in organizations that require high ego involvement. The human relations era of management recognized the need to belong and provided social and recreational groups for employees. But, again, these were largely provided by the company within the larger work environment and not related to the work process itself. Furthermore, as people become more affluent, they no longer need the company to fulfill this need. They can join social groups in the community to have their belonging needs met.

A philosophy of managing by subordinate commitment inhibits the meeting of the need to belong, because the individual must compete with others in the same environment and is thus denied a supportive relationship with them. "In fact, it is possible that personality damage can occur in the same sense in which nervous system damage can occur if levels of social stimulation are inadequate."[4] This can be very destructive. It is only as an organization moves toward managing by team commitment, mutual goal setting and sharing, and team cooperation that the need for belonging can be met within the work process itself.

People stop fighting if fighting gets them into too much trouble with the system. A favorite method of punishment is isolation and the denying of information. This can be a very potent weapon because the people we studied (middle managers and engineers) need information in order to perform effectively, and they depend on the peer group for this. Under management by subordinate commitment, individuals are responsible for collecting their own information. (There are very few briefing sessions.)

The aggressive, intelligent person who enters an organization where advancement is gained by personal contribution is frequently seen as a threat by the peer group. There are many ways in which groups deal with newcomers perceived as threats. The most common is isolation. It is important for newcomers to recognize that too many critical comments or too active a contribution make people defensive, and they may end up as outcasts.

Committed people who will work the long hours that some of these employees worked become terribly lonely. They need someone with whom they can talk . . . someone who will accept and try to understand them.

There are a number of reasons why people are placed in social isolation and denied a sense of belonging. Eventually, people will quit fighting (commit professional suicide) if fighting gets them isolated and into too much trouble with the informal system.

Durkheim found that the suicide rate of a community varies with the extent to which each individual is identified with the social group that controls and defines that person's activities. The more identified the individual is, the less likely to commit suicide.[5] Sainsbury found that suicide rates were highest where both class and spatial mobility are high and lowest where family life and stability prevail. He found loneliness to be a frequent factor in suicides.[6] The successful executive is the one who can prevent subordinates from feeling lost and deserted by the company.[7]

The Need for Recognition and a Sense of Self-Esteem

People also need recognition, self-esteem, and a sense of self-worth. For most people, a sense of self-worth comes through their jobs and the contribution to the world that they make in this way. Many large corporations have recognized and used this to motivate their workers. Efforts to earn more per share for the stockholders have gradually been replaced by such slogans as "Progress is our most important business" or "A better world through research." People need a worthwhile purpose for their lives, and will work harder for such slogans as these than for increasing the profits on a share of stock by a few pennies.

Those we studied were highly oriented toward recognition needs. For the most part, their needs for food, clothing, and shelter had been met, but they did exhibit an intense need for a sense of accomplishment. Top management, consisting of older men with titles and fancy offices, had their own recognition needs sufficiently met. What they offered their subordinates was challenge and opportunities for self-actualization. The subordinates assumed that their recognition needs would be met somewhere along the way. When it became obvious to them that the bosses were not interested in meeting these needs, they began to exhibit the various symptoms of professional suicide.

People need something to do and can stand only a certain amount of enforced idleness and isolation. The inability to get things done is debilitating. Low achievement or having one's achievements unconfirmed results in feelings of low self-worth and guilt, and initiates a descending spiral of ego deterioration. Some suddenly leave the organization when they decide that the recognition and sense of accomplishment they want are not available. Their decisions may be related not to any real lack of achievement, but only to the organization's failure to confirm their achievements. Nothing is less rewarding than unmeasured and unmeasurable progress. Part of the push toward potential professional suicide was trying to prove one's worth in a setting where salary, titles, and authority are downgraded as measures of achievement.

It was almost company policy that individual recognition and status differentiation be depreciated. The personnel department expressed great pride in there being no separate dining room for junior executives. While private parking spaces and more spacious offices were made available to top management, efforts by others to obtain these advantages were ridiculed. Job titles and reporting relationships were semisecret, as every effort was made to keep people happy through "being part of one large family." Because performance reviews (that is, periodic opportunities for recognition and self-esteem) were not given, people did not know how they ranked, and games were played to measure achievement. Highly motivated people want to achieve. If the company does not set the rules for measuring achievement, they will set their own. Such measures as "how close is my office to the boss," "how many hours do I spend in the plant each week," and so on, become ways of gaining a sense of achievement.

From moment to moment we measure and report our standing with ourselves in relation to those around us. This constant reckoning of our value seems to be a reckoning of the value of organizational life itself. If at one point we have had to accept an inevitable and unforgettable defeat, it is all the more necessary to seek a compensating victory elsewhere. Injured self-esteem and acute or chronic states of low visibility almost automatically necessitate securing face-saving grace in some other zone. We are most sensitive and "touchy" about the measurements of others at exactly those points where we most wish to be assured—where the very intensity of our desire to be appreciated makes all but the most convincing of confirmations appear inadequate and disappointing, and where our overanxious self-defense looks like aggression. It is impossible to judge the effects of either wages or other conditions of work apart from the relationships that the work permits with other persons. What every worker knows is that the final joy of working is determined, neither by the worker nor the employer, but by the social standing awarded by fellow citizens.

A sense of self depends to a large extent on emotional relationships with significant others and constant confirmation by them.[8] If we see ourselves as intelligent or handsome, and yet significant others fail to confirm our perceptions by withholding deference or compliments, it becomes difficult to continue to hold onto the self-perception. In the Korean prisoner-of-war camps it was primarily the humiliation, revilement and harassment by cellmates that served to deny the prisoners any role or sense of self. The prisoners could not get *any* positive response (approval or even sustained attention) from other prisoners unless they were willing to assume the "guilty criminal" role. This was a very deteriorating experience and contributed to the high rate of "give-up-itis."

Various studies have shown that the adequacy of their adjustment is directly related to the degree to which individuals perceive themselves as playing significant roles in clearly delineated groups or subgroups that give status to their roles.[9, 10] A high need for approval results in the inhibition of aggressive behavior as a means of coping with a situation, because of the feeling that it could lead to social disapproval. In an experiment with an accomplice who cheated them, subjects with strong needs for approval were willing to continue interacting after having been dealt with in a dastardly fashion, while those with low needs for approval were not.[11] The people we studied had high needs for achievement and low needs for approval. When dealt with in a way they regarded unfair, they tended not to "take it."

Individuals react on the basis of how they view the environment. Individuals with high approval needs select coping strategies based on their evaluation of the behavior needed to preserve the social relationship. If they believe their partners like assertiveness, they behave accordingly.

War does not continue merely because men enjoy the test of supreme moments and thus come to love fighting for fighting's sake. The truth is rather that men everywhere feel the absolute necessity of "saving face," and war offers one of the few arenas where defeat brings to the contestant scarcely less honor than does victory.

One study found an unusually severe incidence of suicide attempts among Cheyenne Indian adolescents.[12] In the early history of the tribe, suicides were rare. When a man became depressed or lost face for some reason, the usual means for dealing with it was to organize a small war party. During the ensuing fight, the warrior would either perform some feat of bravery, which renewed his self-esteem, or engage in a suicidally brave act in which he was killed (although this was not considered suicide).

After they were confined to the reservation, the Indians were forbidden to hold their Sun Dance and other "barbaric" rituals and to hunt the nearly extinct buffalo; and, of course, all fighting between tribes was forbidden. Indian men were forced—for health reasons—to cut their long hair, a symbol of strength; and because they could not support their families, the government set up a welfare program. All this only added to the rapid downward spiral of increasing dependency and loss of self-esteem. Two major symptoms of their cultural deterioration are the high rate of alcoholism and the high incidence of violent injuries, suicide, homicide, and accidents. It appears that as the culturally derived ways of renewing self-esteem and dealing with aggression were systematically lost, aggression began to manifest itself in culturally self-destructive ways.

The main requirements for the development of competent and effective behavior and feelings of inner comfort and acceptance are: expectations of success (hope), motivation to achieve, initiative, and the ability to deal with anxiety.[13] The most important requirement for effective behavior, and central to the whole problem, is self-esteem. It has long been recognized that feelings of personal worth are crucial to human happiness and effectiveness.[14]

In puberty the task of the ego is to assert itself as quickly and as fully as possible by asserting the instinctual drives with which it must make an unconditional alliance. Should the ego fail in this task, suicide offers itself as a paradoxical substitute.[15]

The Need to Grow and Develop
(to Self-Actualize)

People need to grow and develop and to have some sense of self-actualization. The organization under study provided many opportunities for people to study and to learn (evening education programs, tuition aid, and so on) but because little opportunity existed for satisfying recognition–self-esteem needs, people were so preoccupied with these that they could not take full advantage of opportunities for self-actualization.

Maslow has pointed out that human needs are hierarchical. A person does not feel motivated toward self-actualization until security, belonging, and recognition needs have been met. Opportunities for self-actualization are perceived as irrelevant when other more basic needs remain unfulfilled.

Managers whose more basic needs have been met offer subordinates that which would motivate them, apparently unaware that subordinates are at a different level in the needs hierarchy. For a chart defining the various levels of human behavior, the motivational system, the value system, and the managerial system appropriate to each level, see Table 4-1 from Clare Graves.[16]

The Need for a Sense of Purpose

As people become more affluent, they can no longer be motivated so much by the goad of necessity, although crises will be allowed to develop in an effort to create this kind of motivation (motivation by crisis). Herman Kahn believes the biggest problem for the United States and other leading nations in the last third of the century will be the search for meaning and purpose—for an answer to the question, "What's it all about?"[17]

It is important for people to have an interest and purpose in life. We all know people who retired psychologically when they were in their thirties or forties. They may continue working for another two or three decades; but psychologically speaking, they have turned in their uniforms. Perhaps they grew tired, perhaps they were trapped by circumstances, or perhaps they were defeated by self-doubt or fear or cynicism or self-indulgence. Too many people work at a fraction of full capacity because of circumstances

Table 4-1 Levels of Human Behavior

Nature of Existence	Description	Motivational System	Value System	Appropriate Managerial System
	(Higher levels as yet undefined seem to be in the making.)			
7Pacifistic Individualism	Needs "acceptance management." Take me as I am. Requires that the organization be fitted to him. Will build a non-organizationally oriented world and do a passable, but not excellent, job. Ends oriented rather than means oriented.	*Information*	Cognitive	Acceptance and support
6Aggressive Individualism	Disliked by most businessmen—no longer motivated by fear. Will not be told when, how, or where to work. Believes manager's task is to provide the tools to do the job. Excellent producer if he can set the means to the goal. Manage him best by helping him. Highly prone to "professional suicide" because even though an excellent producer, he refuses to conform to the mold.	*Self-Esteem*	Personal	Goal setting without setting means to goals
5Sociocentric Attitudes	Concerned with social rather than personal or material matters. 5,5 style—intermediate concern for people and tasks to 1,9. More to life than hard work. Greatest deterioration is when 5th level managers manage 3rd and 4th level people.	*Belonging* (believes there are other reasons for living than hard work—responsive to groups)	Group mindedness	Participative substitutive 5,5 management

[4] Aggressive Power Seeking	Believes in the power of self. God-given right to change things in the direction he thinks is right.	*Mastery* (believes hard work is the measure of the man)	Power	Personal prescription and hard bargaining
[3] Awakening with Fright	Does not respond to autonomy and participation—chooses autocracy. Tries to construct an orderly, predictable, and unchanging world to deal with the flood of stimulation. Lives in a moralistically prescribed world.	*Order* (believes in a moral duty to do one's best)	Constrictive	Moralistic and prescriptive 9,1 management
[2] Animistic Existence	Individual beginning to awake. Needs very close and immediate supervision, force will work if not in conflict with taboos. (Force will not work with first-level people.)	*Survival*	Totem and Taboo	Simple demonstration, force
[1] Autistic Behavior	Man's energies concerned with staying alive. Sees few problems beyond sustenance, illness, reproduction, and disputes. In no state for productive effort, management must give and give in hopes growth will occur.	*Physiological*	Amoral	Close care and nurturing

SOURCE: Clare W. Graves, "Deterioration of Work Standards," *Harvard Business Review*, Sept.–Oct. 1966, pp. 117–128.

that could be altered. In this country life during their first 25 years has been so future-oriented that for many of our young people the present has little reality and only the future is real. They live with their eye on the upward curve of their own careers and fortunes. Then, in middle life, the future vanishes. The mid-life crisis occurs with the realization that the future is limited, life does not go on forever, and if you are not now getting what you need you had better do something about it.

Personnel departments frequently try to establish trust and concern before establishing superordinate goals. To establish trust or concern requires the establishment of contact. But experiments by Sherif (discussed further in Chapter 6) show that to establish contact without superordinate goals creates greater antagonism and mistrust. In the absence of clearly stated organizational goals and periodic evaluation of individual performance, individuals find other (less organizationally relevant) ways of satisfying "recognition hunger."[18]

Spitz has shown that infants who are not handled or stimulated develop apathetic states he calls "mirasmus," and eventually die.[19] S. Levine found that gentle handling and painful electric shocks were equally effective in promoting the health of rats, while being isolated and ignored was harmful to them.[20] In other words, health requires interaction; and almost any interaction (even painful) is preferable to none. When an organization does not establish a positive structure within which people can interact (such as goal setting and performance reviews), then, in the interest of health, people will establish their own modes of interacting. A common interactional mode in industrial settings is crisis stimulation.

With the exception of predatory people oriented primarily to their own survival, most people in organizations need organizational objectives toward which to direct their efforts. They want a sense of purpose to their lives beyond the satisfaction of personal needs. Like generators, achieving people tend to spin apart without a load of some significance.

An individual with an achieving orientation in an organization where purpose and the means to legitimate recognition are kept nebulous is inevitably frustrated. It was the lack of a sense of organizational purpose (beyond the vague admonition to "grow" and "make more profit") and the absence of a structure to define and coordinate activities that was found to be so destructive to the bright, young, energetic people in the organization studied.

The Need for a Structure from Which to View the World

In the desire to give people greater freedom for self-actualization, efforts have been made to remove organizational structure; however, instead of providing more freedom, it has in many ways provided less. People feel as though they have been dropped into a jungle. Their uncoordinated efforts to provide some kind of order to this jungle *on their own* are very frustrating; and yet order is needed to help accomplish those things the individual cannot do entirely alone. Lack of order makes many people frightened, apprehensive, unsure, and even more inhibited. In the psychotherapeutic treatment of children raised in a free, too-permissive atmosphere, completely lacking rules and regulations, we find that these children develop great constriction because they do not know in what areas they are really free to move when all areas are declared free. They cope with the anxiety of not enough rules by becoming overcontrolled and constricted.

In a highly complex organization, it appears to us that some freedoms come from the presence of structure. Some ordering of the many variables in a situation is needed so that one is not overpowered by the tremendous complexity of it all. Some structuring of relationships frees the minds of employees from having to be concerned with "everything" and makes mental energy available for more creative and organizationally useful pursuits. "An adult human must have some sort of viable role and identity which permits him to organize his own behavior and make meaningful contact with others in his social environment."[21] The free-floating predators enjoy the opportunity to roam through the organization, freely taking what they will for their own gratification; but dedicated individuals committed to organizationally significant tasks find themselves hampered by an unstructured environment. Freedom is not the absence, but rather the acceptance and integration, of rules and regulations.

Studies of chickens and monkeys show that the establishment of hierarchy in groups is necessary to form a cooperative, stable society.[22] A hierarchy or pecking order in most organizations is established by the line chart, from which individuals can quickly determine their positions relative to others and can decide to whom they must pay attention, whose requests bear most weight, and whom they can ignore.

At any moment an individual's behavior is the result of at least four different kinds of simultaneous appraisals:

1. An appraisal of task requirements
2. An appraisal of one's own role
3. An appraisal of environmental constraints
4. An assessment of the range of actions one might take and their potential results for one's own short-range and long-range goals.

Appraisal of these factors is complicated at best; but when the organization keeps this information intentionally vague, it creates additional stress for the individual. When line charts are kept hidden (as in management by subordinate commitment) in the belief that anarchical societies are most free, much time is spent in meetings (and outside of meetings) trying to establish one's position. Arguments are followed carefully and all kinds of innuendos are carefully examined in an effort to determine who is most in favor.

Cultures with high degrees of social mobility have high rates of mental illness. Organizations without established and visible hierarchies, where people have difficulty finding out where they stand, have high rates of stress, conflict and "professional suicide/murder."

The Destructive Effects of Severe Frustration

Studies of stress have shown that the first phase is an alarm reaction or initial shock (in which resistance is lowered); then comes a countershock phase (in which defense mechanisms become active), followed by a third stage during which maximum adaptation occurs. Should the stress persist or the defensive reactions prove ineffective, a stage of exhaustion is finally reached, during which the adaptive mechanisms collapse.[23]

The most healthy and reality-oriented way to deal with frustration is to expend creative energy in overcoming the obstacle. The employees in the study did this, up to a point; but when their frustrations became too severe, they adapted other less healthy mechanisms for dealing with their problems. When the pressures for solving problems build up and solutions are not readily available, failure may introduce tension. People may become severely frustrated rather than employing creative problem-solving behavior. The major nonconstructive mechanisms for dealing with frustration are resignation, aggression, regression, and fixation.

In resignation, individuals give up and refuse to work on problems, sometimes by leaving the organization and sometimes by just refusing to exert themselves in situations which appear incapable of solution. Some of those we studied acted this way.

In aggression, individuals deal with frustration through some kind of attack on the boss, the project, or the system. They may storm out of meetings, destroy papers, or write nasty letters. We no longer punch people in the nose, but we may attack another's reputation, which can be even more severely damaging.

In regression, individuals revert to childish or even babyish behavior. People become highly suggestible under severe frustration and may accept contracts and tolerances that they would not otherwise accept. Managers who have difficulty remembering things and making decisions, who engage in broad and unreasonable generalizations, and who form blind loyalties for particular persons or organizations may show the symptoms of regression.

When escape routes are seen as completely blocked, a reaction to extreme danger can be immobilization. Marshall found that, in amphibious attacks during World War II, immobility in the face of enemy fire was a common response. With the sea at their backs and no place to run even if they had been capable of movement, soldiers sat dumbly in the line of fire with their minds blanked out and their fingers too nerveless even to hold a weapon.[24] Analyses of mine and submarine disasters have shown that panic occurs only when possibilities of escape seem closed.

In fixation (or repetition compulsion), individuals appear compelled to continue activities that have no real value or are even destructive, repeating them over and over in spite of the fact that they will accomplish nothing. Maier comments that a rat, if severely frustrated, can be made to bang its head against a locked door hundreds of times without ever trying the unlocked door next to it.[25] College students can have their ability to learn a new problem reduced 50 percent by being subjected to mild frustration beforehand.

The range of stress to which human beings can be subjected and still survive is vast. The struggle for survival today is no longer on a physical battleground, but rather on a psychological battlefield where the weapons are anxiety (lack of security), exclusion (no sense of belonging), and being degraded and demeaned (denied recognition for work well done). Defeat frequently results from overcommitment, which causes mental and physical exhaustion from the psychological stress of isolation, unmet needs, and humiliation.

A frequent cause of suicide is that the behavior necessary for survival demands unacceptable violations of a person's norms. One of the reasons survivors of concentration camps are so reluctant to talk about their experiences is that to survive they did things they could not approve of. Their very survival is proof of guilt. But obviously the same conditions affect different people quite differently. The degree to which a situation degrades, demeans, and shames a person is a highly individual matter. Internal reactions rather than the specific circumstances produce the devastating effect. (And the knowledge that someone cares and understands helps one continue.)

A group of highly competitive managers, all about the same age, competing for the same jobs, may have difficulties in cooperating, even under the threat of not surviving. Group survival is a natural objective towards which people will organize when all seem to have a good chance of succeeding, provided there is leadership and concerted action toward a common goal. However, in situations where it becomes apparent that there is not enough for all, group cooperation quickly breaks down. Severe competition between workers makes it difficult for them to form coalitions of mutual support, even when this is essential for their survival and for the achievement of necessary organizational goals.

Under conditions of psychological starvation and recognition hunger, the quest for approval becomes all-important, and many social constraints and codes of morality lose their force. The breakdown in social, intellectual, and cultural controls contributes to professional suicide by reducing the cooperative functioning of the group, which is so necessary for the survival of any considerable proportion of its members. The breakdown of control and the submission to more expedient measures also hinder individuals' use of intelligence, planning, and insight for their own survival and for effective group functioning. Where the sustenance that an environment can provide may be less than is necessary to maintain all the members of a group, some may nonetheless survive and even prosper while others perish. That some do survive and prosper is not necessarily proof that the organizational climate is benign, although those in control often point to the survival of some as proof that the organization cannot be "all that bad."

Professional suicide appears most frequently during the third year. Many despair of achieving what they want in what appears to them by now to be absolutely hopeless circumstances. Peers will sometimes ask, "Why don't you leave?" But with self-confidence undermined and egos shaken, they do not have the strength even to leave unless a crisis is precipitated for them. The answer to the question, "Why don't you leave?" is comparable to the answer to the question, "Why don't you commit suicide?" "Because of family, because it would be weak, because it is irreversible. . . ."

Notes

1. Elsie Boulding, *Conflict Management in Organizations* (Ann Arbor: Foundation for Research on Human Behavior, 1961), p. 54.

2. Abraham Maslow, *Toward a Psychology of Being* (Princeton, N.J.: Van Nostrand, 1962).

3. Basic human needs according to Fromm:
   (1) To be related to others through productive love
   (2) To be transcendent; that is, to create rather than destroy

(3)   To have roots; that is, to feel that one belongs to or is part of the world or the brotherhood of man

(4)   To have a sense of personal or individual identity; to be unique

(5)   To have a frame of reference in terms of which to perceive and understand the world.
From Erik Fromm, *The Sane Society* (New York: Reinhart, 1955), pp. 27–66.

4.   E. H. Schein, I. Schneier, and C. H. Barker, *Coercive Persuasion* (Norton, New York, 1961).

5.   Emile Durkheim, *Suicide* (New York; Free Press, 1951), p. 248.

6.   Peter Sainsbury, *Suicides in London: An Ecological Study* (London: Chapman and Hall, 1955).

7.   Harry Levinson, *The Exceptional Executive,* Cambridge, Mass.: Harvard, 1968.

8.   E. H. Schein, "Interpersonal Communication, Group Solidarity, and Social Influence," *Sociometry,* 1960, pp. 148–161.

9.   E. L. Scott, "Perceptions of Organization and Leadership Behavior," ONR Contr. N 6 ori-17, Columbus: Ohio State University, 1952.

10.   E. P. Torrance, "A Theory of Leadership and Interpersonal Behavior Under Stress," in L. Petrullo & B. M. Bass (eds.) *Leadership and Interpersonal Behavior* (New York: Holt, Rinehart and Winston, 1961), pp. 100–117.

11.   L. K. Conn and D. P. Crowne, "Instigation to Aggression, Emotional Arousal and Defense Emulation," *Journal of Personality,* 32, 1964, pp. 163–179.

12.   Larry H. Dizmang, M. D., "Suicide Among the Cheyenne Indians," *Bulletin of Suicidology,* July 1967, National Institute of Mental Health, pp. 8–11.

13.   Stanley Coopersmith, "Studies in Self-Esteem," *Scientific American,* February 1968, pp. 96–106.

14.   The psychologist, William James; the philosopher, George Herbert Mead; and the psychologist, Alfred Adler, to mention a few.

15.   Gregory Zilboorg, "Considerations on Suicide with Particular Reference to that of the Young," *American Journal of Orthopsychiatry,* 7, 1937, pp. 15–31.

16.   Clare W. Graves, "Deterioration of Work Standards," *Harvard Business Review,* September–October, 1966, pp. 117–128.

17.   *Business Week,* March 11, 1967, pp. 114–118.

18.   Eric Berne, *Games People Play* (New York: Grove Press, 1964).

19.   Rene Spitz, "Hospitalism: Genesis of Psychiatric Conditions in Early Childhood," *Psychoanalytic Study of the Child,* 1: 53–74, 1945.

20.   S. Levin, "Stimulation in Infancy," *Scientific American,* 202, May 1960, pp. 80–86.

21. E. H. Schein, I. Schneier, and C. H. Barker, *Coercive Persuasion* (New York: Norton, 1961).

22. Joseph P. Coogan, "Simian Society Research at Yerkes Primate Center," *S K & F Psychiatric Reporter,* May–June 1968, 38, pp. 3–6.

23. Hans Selye, *The Stress of Life* (New York: McGraw-Hill, 1956).

24. L. A. Marshall, "Men Against Fire," *The Infantry Journal,* Washington, 1947.

25. Norman R. F. Maier, *Psychology in Industry* (Boston: Houghton Mifflin, 1965).

five

Organizational Characteristics Contributing to the Suicide Process

Unless we cope with the ways in which modern society oppresses the individual, we shall lose the creative spark that both renews societies and men.[1]

When human skills go to waste or are allowed to rust away for lack of honing, you can blame it largely on organizational structure.[2]

In addition to characteristics of individuals that predispose them to professional suicide, this study also found a number of organizational characteristics that contribute to the suicide process. While it would not be correct to imply that the environment or the organization's leadership actually encouraged suicides, it is necessary to point out that certain organizational procedures and values contain stresses that impel certain people toward professional suicide.

For countless eons, people have been concerned with physical survival, but today—at least in America—the problem of mere physical survival has been largely overcome by advances in medicine and improvements in nutrition and the standard of living. Today's problem, instead, is emotional and psychological survival —as is all too obvious in the high rate of admissions to mental hospitals (one person in ten will spend some time in a mental hospital), the high divorce rate (in the United States 50 percent of marriages end in divorce), and the high suicide rate (after automobile accidents—which may have a suicide component—suicide is the major cause of death for Americans age 15 to 19). The criteria for physical survival are relatively well known in terms of body temperature, weight, and so on. Although the criteria for emotional and psychological survival are much less well known, psychological survival appears to be based on the availability of such things as supportive relationships, a sense of belonging, occasional self-confirmation by others, and recognition.

In this section some of the organizational characteristics that create and encourage professional suicide will be discussed. These include:

The stress of ambiguous situations and "not knowing"

The lack of specific organizational goals and objectives

The lack of a plan for achieving goals

Confusion over "rules of the game"

The lack of team building

The lack of evaluation, criticism, and individual performance reviews

The lack of an objective reward system based on organizational results

The stress of anxiety as a motivator

The stress of competition as a motivator

The stress of guilt as a motivator

In addition to a number of other miscellaneous characteristics that contribute to the suicide process, this section will discuss certain broader philosophical issues such as:

An organizational orientation of survival instead of growth

Problems of interpersonal competence

The effect of certain existential beliefs on management policy

Problems in present organizational strategies for meeting people's needs

The Stress of Ambiguous Situations and "Not Knowing"

A major problem for the young employees in this study was the stress of not knowing and not being able to find out. For the most part, it was extremely difficult to determine (1) specific organizational goals and how they relate to me, (2) the plan for meeting these goals, (3) my charter of responsibility and authority for contributing to meeting these goals, (4) the most effective organizational use of my energies, (5) how my performance is being evaluated, (6) what mistakes I am making that I should correct, (7) what I am doing right, and (8) how any of this relates to my being rewarded and my needs being met.

It is, of course, self-evident that over the past 40 years organizational life in the industrial environment, as well as in other settings, has become vastly more complicated. Confronted with increased complexity, management—operating under a philosophy of subordinate commitment—has maintained that the subordinate should either ignore this increased complexity or resolve it on his own. They say, "We must find men who can live with ambiguity." Yet, ambiguous organizations are unlikely to be as successful as those where the leadership can effectively channel employee energy toward organizationally relevant goals.

A study done in one department of the organization found almost complete confusion over what a "good job" was and little agreement on how organizationally valued were certain kinds of behavior.[3] This problem seemed to penetrate most levels of the organization under study.

In a study done among the top 19 managers in the organization, they said the major impediments to their becoming more effective were:

6: The lack of policy, decision making, and direction

4: The way in which we are organized

3: Communication problems and interpersonal "hang-ups"

2: A feeling my job is not very important

1: Knowledge problems

3: No answer [4]

Called by such high-sounding words as "freedom" and "opportunity," ambiguity has become an important factor in the American managerial system. Coping with ambiguity has become a common stress that managers have to deal with.

When placed in ambiguous, unclear situations, small children make efforts to have limits set for them by becoming anxious and destructive or by withdrawing into frightened passivity as a result of unsureness what is all right for them to do. Some adults respond in similar fashion. Admonitions not to let it bother you have little effect.

The Lack of Specific Organizational Goals and Objectives

Almost any company can solve 75 percent of its business problems if it will just ask itself the basic question, "What in the hell are we trying to do?"[5]

In organizations based on self-actualization, individual competitiveness, and a management philosophy of subordinate commitment, the groups which form and the efforts undertaken tend to be based on personal advantage with an everyone-for-himself atmosphere. If not directed toward organizational goals clearly stated, energies become directed toward personal goals. Mutual interest cliques form which hoard organizational resources to disburse to those who provide the individual with personal gratification of one kind or another. With organizational goals undefined, resources are disbursed in meeting personal goals rather than rewarding the achievement of organizational goals. Without a process within the system for integrating personal and organizational goals, organizational resources get wasted on a multiplicity of conflicting and organizationally irrelevant efforts. Without defined organizational goals, the rules of the game support psychological one-upsmanship. Management's answer to its own lack of goalsetting and planning was to admonish subordinates to be more committed and to do on their own, without direction, that which needed to be done. What needed to be done was hard to determine by oneself.

Lack of clearly stated policy provides room for staff people to maneuver and to provide greater benefits for friends than for nonfriends. While in the short run this provides a way to influence people in the organization, in the long run such favoritism eventually becomes obvious, with resulting disenchantment and dissatisfaction with the organization that continues to permit this.

There are some advantages to the organization in developing and maintaining ambiguity. Among them are that:

1. Ambiguity provides a ready scapegoat for managerial incompetence. As one manager is reported to have said, "You have the authority to do anything which in retrospect turns out to have been right." If the responsibility for tasks is poorly defined and a subordinate gets into trouble, the subordinate takes the blame. This can be an advantage to managers who want to maintain their position of control even though unfamiliar with the new technology of the business.

2. Ambiguity makes people anxious, so that they put in many extra hours. The problem is that subordinates eventually catch on that working hard because of anxiety is not much fun and they quit, or retire on the job, or in some other way become suicides. For the first few years, however, the organization gets a great deal of extra effort from them. A highly anxious state produces lots of "footwork," but is not conducive to solving problems creatively. In the mass production of relatively standard items, footwork may be functional, but the employees in this study could make the greatest contribution by finding nontraditional creative solutions to problems. It is difficult to be creative when anxious.

3. Providing ambiguous charters is one way of having many people (in the short term) work on the same problem.

4. With lots of ambiguity in the system, difficult, imponderable problems are left with subordinates. Managers can avoid facing administrative problems and their own inadequacies by proclaiming, "Don't bring me problems; bring me solutions."

In an effort to create an atmosphere where people could be more free and in an effort to increase opportunities for self-actualization, organizational goals and structure were hidden and people were encouraged to do what they wanted. However, instead of more freedom, for many it seems to have created less freedom. What actually happened was that it suddenly became legitimate to actualize yourself at someone else's expense. No charters were sacred. Anyone who wanted anything someone else had was welcome to try to take it. A highly competitive environment developed between helpers and helpees. Individual employees responded by building moats around their territories and admitting no help except as a last resort. Admitting help frequently led to the helper staying to take over and the helpee being left out in the cold.

So much energy went into the competitive struggle of protecting what one had that there was little left for creative tasks. An obvious alternative to this situation is to: (1) establish superordinate goals, (2) provide group recognition for contributions toward these goals, and (3) downplay individual self-actualization in favor of team building and group actualization.

The purposeful direction of organization activity requires a substantial amount of energy from members of the system. For goal-directed activity to be possible, certain conditions must be met. There must be:

1. Physical facilities
2. Supplies and financial support
3. Physical and psychological safety
4. A sense of organizational and community identity
5. A sense of esteem

In summary, the lack of clearly stated, specific organizational goals makes it hard for individuals interested in helping the organization to channel their energies in organizationally useful ways. Without specific organizational goals and objectives it is difficult for aggressive individuals interested in accomplishment to gain the sense of accomplishment and self-esteem that comes from achieving something regarded as organizationally important.

A major problem in many organizations is the lack of an organizational overseer, someone (or some group) with an overall concept of the business, who is aware of the direction of the business (who should be doing what) and who can legislate organizational priorities on the basis of organizational needs rather than political pressure brought to bear by subunits. For management to do this, certain kinds of skills are necessary, which we will discuss further later on.

> Results are obtained by exploiting opportunities, not by solving problems. All one can hope to get by solving a problem is to restore normality. . . . Resources to produce results must be allocated to opportunities rather than to problems. . . . The pertinent question is not how to do things right, but how to find the right things to do and to concentrate resources and efforts on them.[6]

The Lack of a Plan for Achieving Goals

> The greatest foresight consists in determining beforehand the time of trouble. For the provident there are no mischances and for the careful no narrow escapes. We must not put off thought till we are up to the chin in mire. Gratian

In the organization under study, perhaps because so many variables were unknown, there was great reluctance to plan and set priorities. Multiple demands for limited resources resulted in no clear guidelines to which allocation was organizationally most relevant. Decisions left up to the individuals involved were often made on the basis of personal interest or the implied power of the person making a request, rather than the good of the organization.

When responsibility is assumed rather than assigned, there develops a natural scapegoating process by which the manager has the advantage of being able to blame anything that goes wrong on the subordinate.

Lack of structure creates problems for the subordinate, because the organization views efforts to assume responsibility without authority as usurpation of something not legitimate to take. Nothing upsets people so much as having something they think is theirs taken over by someone else. This is especially true of a job function. Existential management, management by exception, and management by subordinate commitment, claiming to build on the theories of Douglas McGregor, have deemphasized position, titles, charters of responsibility, and reporting relationships.

In the organization under study, line charts were intentionally made very difficult to obtain, and reporting relationships were kept purposefully vague and poorly defined. The official reason given was the effort to create a flat organization where responsibility would be widely distributed. Another explanation, by those disenchanted with this style of management, was the desire to placate everyone and the unwillingness to confront individuals with the basic realities of their roles. The result of this role ambiguity was that covertly, and sometimes quite openly, much subordinate time was spent in subtle competitive efforts to establish positions in the pecking order. Organizational level and the person to whom one reports are important because this determines who one works with, from whom to expect help, and who one's peers are; not to mention the influence upon salary level.

The organization was expected to function through the informal system of personal relationships rather than the formal system of reporting relationships. Because it lacks structure, the organization became extremely fluid. Organizational holes were filled in almost immediately, like "taking your hand out of a bucket of water." This created a sense of impermanence, and generated anxiety and insecurity.

Subordinates were taught that competence (by definition) would make itself felt. And if competence did not make itself felt, the problem lay with the individual, not the system. This, of course, nicely avoided the system confronting itself with its own inadequacies. While there are persons who can move into an organization and gradually take over, I doubt that this is an appropriate definition for competence. For if competence is to be expressed, it needs a function and a role. For competence to be perceived, it must have an organizationally significant function. When competence is operationally defined as the ability to control others or to get needs met through others, in a highly competitive environment with superordinate goals unestablished, there is real advantage in being uncooperative with peers, because this keeps rivals from being seen as competent.

Waldman points out that "neurotic conduct is an outcome of a lack of meaningful action possibilities within the social framework."[7] Most of the suicides in this study were caught in this bind.

Ostensibly, we hope for freedom and individuality, but at the same time we strip away the very supports necessary to nurture freedom. "In the name of humanism, release from constraints of tradition is a rarefied medium too difficult to endure."[8] The family and other associative groups that traditionally supplied a sense of purpose, values, and ends are now rendered impotent by the emphasis on release from all constraints.

Reluctance to disseminate line charts, lack of clearly defined authority relationships, and lack of an organizationally defined hierarchical structure mean that individuals spend much time jockeying for position and social advantage. They also think they must spend much time protecting their prerogatives. Prerogatives not officially defined can be informally assumed by someone else if not continually protected, resulting in loss of organization esteem and self-esteem.

Mechanic has pointed out that there is considerable evidence that *lack* of constraint is more likely than constraint to lead to suicide.[9] A hypothesis by Henry and Short is that constraint leads to outward aggression, while those under less constraint are more likely to express aggression inwardly.[10] And Biderman has shown that suicide rates are usually exceptionally low in situations of extremely oppressive captivity.[11]

Conjectures as to why suicide rates should be low in extraordinary captivity situations are that: (1) The pressure of immediate demands causes much mobilization to meet moment-by-moment requirements, so that feelings of hopelessness and futility fail to get translated into action; (2) the general apathy that characterizes individuals under such conditions causes difficulty in mobilizing themselves for so decisive an act.

Without role definition and structure, individuals dedicated to improving the organization may become martyred messiahs in an ill-conceived cause by trying to satisfy every demand made on them.[12] Unless roles and goals are well defined in accordance with the reality of the resources and energies available, an unfeeling, uncaring organization will undermine and ultimately destroy the individual. The management did not recognize or accept this responsibility.

Confusion Over Rules of the Game

A characteristic seriously affecting the lives of its people is the organization's value system and its expectations about how work and organizational goals are to be accomplished. The climate of an organization is largely determined by its prevailing assumptions about the fundamental nature of man and its expectations about how people are going to work together.[13] Traditionally, most industrial organizations have had a bureaucratic utilitarian philosophy and have operated under a value system that stressed bureaucratic values.[14]

Their interest in developing a more effective and profitable company led business leaders to continually search for more effective values (defined in terms of organizational innovation and production). Industrial leaders were impressed by the tremendous amounts of work for small remuneration that churches and certain other organizations dedicated to idealistic goals were able to obtain from their members. Trying to tap more of the potential of their workers, many of the more progressive industries began to develop idealistic values and purposes in addition to their business ones. There are big advantages to having employees dedicated to their work; and although there are sometimes problems in getting them undedicated, the advantages of a commitment philosophy of management for employees appeared obvious.

A value system thought to be more effective than the bureaucratic utilitarian approach for running certain kinds of organizations is a system which might be called the "commitment approach" (see table 5-1.) In the organization studied in this report, many employees were confused about whether the organization had a bureaucratic, utilitarian value system (where I am a sucker if I do not push for raises and titles) or a dedicated commitment philosophy (where I raise questions in management's mind about my commitment and dedication if I push for something for myself).

Historically, a philosophy of commitment probably entered business through research, development and engineering departments, where the ratio of college-educated people and Ph.D.'s to non-college-educated people was high. Many came from educa-

Table 5-1   Two Philosophical Systems for Achieving Organizational Results

Bureaucratic Utilitarian Approach to Organizational Tasks	Commitment Approach to Organizational Tasks
1. I work for the organization because of what it does for me—when what it does for me drops below a certain level, I leave.	1. I work for the organization not for what it does for me, but because I believe in the cause it stands for and working there gives me a chance to work with others toward a personally important objective.
2. Authority for my job resides in the organizational box I currently occupy. If someone else fills that box, the responsibility and authority become theirs. If I perform the duties of another box, its occupant has a right to be angry about the usurpation and to call for clarification from the next box up.	2. Authority for my job resides not in the job title or the organizational box I occupy currently, but in my ability to contribute toward the common goal. Job titles and boxes may be periodically reshuffled to reflect my contribution.
3. You exert influence and further your own ends by controlling money and people—the more money and people to whom you can say no, the more powerful you are.	3. Knowledge and capability are power—not boxes and reporting relationships.
	4. A "scramble" system is in effect—you may go anywhere inside or outside the system for help. The important thing is to solve the problem and get results.
4. This is a hierarchical system. You go to your boss and "through channels" for help.	
5. Rewards are based on seniority and on not disrupting the system.	5. Rewards are based on commitment and getting results. This frequently disrupts the system.
6. Men work on what is organizationally most relevant. It is the boss's job to define this.	6. Men work on what they want to do and are responsible for developing their own goals with or without their boss's help

tional institutions which were characterized more by a philosophy of commitment than a hard bargaining, bureaucratic, utilitarian philosophy. (The progression from transactional to committed relationships is gradual, and if it appears here that they are dichotomous, it is only for ease in discussing two points of view that in practice are on a continuum.)

Many suicides began to occur when individuals began to realize that although a commitment approach to organizational tasks was evolving and being taught, a bureaucratic approach was being practiced by those in managerial control of the organization. As employees discovered that organizational rewards were based not on commitment nor on the results accomplished (because these were difficult to measure and time-consuming to define) but rather on seniority and having contacts at the top, they felt cheated, angry, and resentful. They felt they had been lied to and duped. In time, these feelings caused decreased effectiveness and eventual identification as professional suicides.

A major problem in the organization studied was confusion over the rapidly evolving rules of the game and the problem of how to go about working together. For many years there had been an effort to substitute more modern, behavioral science values for the traditional bureaucratic rules of the game, which include:

1. A division of labor based on functional specialization
2. A well-defined hierarchy of authority
3. A system of rules covering the rights and duties of employees
4. A system of procedures for dealing with work situations
5. Impersonality of interpersonal relations
6. Promotion and selection based on technical competence[15]

There are a number of problems associated with the traditional bureaucratic system, some of which are:

1. Bureaucracy does not adequately allow for personal growth and the development of mature personalities.
2. It develops conformity and "groupthink."
3. It does not take into account the informal organization and the emergent and unanticipated problems.

4.   Its systems of control and authority are hopelessly outdated.

5.   It has no adequate juridical process.

6.   It does not possess adequate means for resolving differences and conflict among ranks and, most particularly, among functional groups.

7.   Communication and innovative ideas are thwarted or distorted because of hierarchical divisions.

8.   The full human resources of bureaucracy are not used because of mistrust, fear of reprisals, etc.

9.   It cannot assimilate the influx of new technology or scientists entering the organization.

10.   It modifies the personality structure so that employees become dull, gray, conditioned "organization men."[16]

The more modern behavioral science values, which the organization was trying to establish, are:

1.   Full and free communication, regardless of rank and power

2.   Reliance on consensus, rather than on the more customary forms of coercion or compromise, to manage conflict

3.   Influence based on technical competence and knowledge rather than on the vagaries of personal whims or prerogatives of power

4.   An atmosphere that permits and even encourages emotional expression as well as task-oriented acts

5.   A basically human bias—one that accepts the inevitability of conflict between the organization and the individual, but is willing to cope with and mediate this conflict on rational grounds[17]

Without organizational objectives, the rules of the game become manipulation and pressure. There is no logical way to assess the organizational relevance of certain actions, so people respond to personal interest, personal goals, and pressure. The result is an organization running off in all directions—amoeba-like, able to pull itself together only in times of crisis. Until the project reached phase V there was no concentrated overall effort to explain and implement the behavioral science values. Under management by subordinate commitment, educational efforts were piecemeal, on an individual-by-individual basis. This left most of the people in the organization confused and anxious about what was expected. The admonitions, "be committed" and "do what you feel needs to be done," were not very helpful. With little clarification of the rules of the game by those in leadership positions, people worked at cross purposes, with inevitable antagonism and inefficiency.

One of the ways to ingratiate yourself with a system is to find apologies for its faults. Many philosophies have been developed in an attempt to make poor management palatable to those who have to work with it. Chief among them is what has come to be known as "management by exception" or "existential management." This refers to a philosophy of management characterized by: (1) doing nothing until one is in trouble, (2) expecting subordinates to solve all the organizational problems, and (3) avoiding responsibility by getting subordinates to accept total responsibility, including taking all blame for things that do not go well.

In many organizations there are two philosophies for managing—one for subordinates and another for oneself. The standards we idealize for others are different from those we find practical for ourselves. When subordinates begin to realize this, it affects the quality as well as the quantity of their work.

We found in this organization that the standards that were idealized and taught were different from those that bosses seemed to find practical for themselves. When subordinates became aware of this, a "credibility gap" developed that hastened the suicide process. New employees were told: (1) You are to commit yourself to a task. (2) We consider titles or roles relatively unimportant. (3) We have many problems; the measure of your capability will be your ability to solve them. Anyone can do it with all the authority and resources needed—your challenge will be to do it without these. (4) If you are truly capable, you can work without a charter, a title, and authority—if you are capable, you can gain the organization's cooperation on your own without direction or assistance from me.

Management held out to subordinates the belief that the organization was a "tabula rasa" on which individuals—if capable—could write their own tickets. This psychological contract, vaguely defined and placing a great deal of stress and responsibility on individuals, became the source of potential suicide for them.

Management taught that the way to involve people was to offer them opportunities to confront challenges and for self-actualization. Responsibilities were only vaguely assigned, the assumption being that they would be eagerly sought by committed people. While management preached that committed people would move ahead without desiring ego-satisfying rewards, authority and the prerogatives of status were retained by those in managerial control.

Stan Herman has pointed out that the modern idea of manipulation is to get people to do what you want because they want to do it, or because they like you, or because they think you are wise, or because they want to be part of your team, or because of any other noncoercive reason.[18] For the practitioner of modern manipulation, "participation" has been translated into an elaborately advertised advocacy of allowing subordinates the privilege of choosing between equally inconsequential alternatives within the framework of unimportant situations.

Subordinates were told their futures were based on the measure of their commitment, and for a time subordinates worked eagerly on the basis of this promise. Only after some time with the organization did the individual begin to discover that people were "offered opportunities," moved from job to job and challenge to challenge—but only very rarely did anyone ever really move upward. To ask about the absence of upward movement was regarded with suspicion, as something committed people did not do, and a violation of management's expectation (see Table 5-2).

Another area of confusion is about what subordinates can do to have an influence upward. Table 5-3 shows ways by which subordinates try to influence the organization and the results of each.

The Lack of Team Building

When the boss does not have the skills to develop a smoothly functioning team, which can reach mutually-arrived-at collabora-

Table 5-2 Some Areas of Management—Subordinate Misunderstanding and Conflict

Promises Held Out	What Seemed to Actually Happen
1. If you do good work, you will be rewarded.	1. The only way you get rewarded is by threatening to quit.
2. If you develop a product, you will be placed in charge of your own division or works.	2. When a product becomes successful enough, it is given to manufacturing, and you are sent back to develop another product.
3. We want people who will seize responsibility.	3. The result of seizing responsibility is: (1) you get more work to do, (2) people see you as a threat and get mad at you, (3) you get less cooperation from the organization.
4. I want you to push me (management) for the things you feel need to be done.	4. Management talks to you less and less.
5. Results count.	5. Results are not as important as how your boss or your boss's boss feel about you (unless your boss can take credit for what you do—too many results may make him look bad).
6. I want to know what you think regardless of how unflattering it may be.	6. If what you think is not flattering, you end up being punished.
7. We are in a rapidly expanding corporation, where there is lots of opportunity for you to get ahead.	7. We are in an area that is static or declining, and there are in fact few opportunities here.

tive decisions, a handy expedient is to appoint a program manager, whose assignment is to complete without authority the tasks that the boss has not been able to do with authority. The rate of professional suicide among these managers is obviously very high.

When tasks become so emphasized that people begin to lose

Table 5-3 Effectiveness of Subordinates' Efforts to Influence Management

Type of Effort	Ineffective	Effective but Risky	Effective but Time-Consuming	Effective and Efficient
1. Memos and written proposals	X			
2. Emphatic statements of "I want," a. without implied threat	X			
b. with implied threat		X		
3. Communication to boss of the person you are trying to influence		X		
4. Grass roots movements—build power blocks via the grapevine			X	
5. Grab a current crisis or create one and use it to influence				X
6. Spend informal time with influential people (Become a good golfer, get invited to foursomes)			X	
7. Set organizational goals and develop systems to evaluate ideas relative to contribution to goals			X	
8. Find sponsor who in exchange for credit will champion your projects upward				X

their concern for others and for quality, organizations may impose a matrix overlay, with a program manager responsible for tasks and a functional head responsible for people and quality. The resolution of conflicting job demands is then delegated to the subordinate, who makes decisions based on personal interest rather than on organizational priorities. As a result, people become more and more burdened with making decisions for which their information about the business is inadequate.

A study by Shils and Janowitz of German troops who continued to fight even when they knew the war was over showed that it was group ties and comparisons with others within primary groups that made men continue to fight for a lost cause.[19] Social comparisons set the limits on what possible defense and coping techniques will be used by making clear the values relevant to approaching particular kinds of crises. With no standards, people work harder and harder for a time, out of a desire for some sense of accomplishment. But after a while they may perpetuate failure as a standard against which to work.

When an organization is growing obsolete, in that it is having increasing difficulty meeting the demands of reality, there are several strategies for explaining this situation to the organization's leadership higher up. The first reasons given are usually those over which management has the least control: subordinates' personalities (for example, their inability to be motivated) and technical capabilities, or the external situation (problems in the market environment). Then, if pressure for improvement increases (because the problems are increasing), there is movement toward diagnosing the problem in ways more likely to be corrected because management has more control over them; for instance, management's training and skill in dealing with people.

There is a need for leadership to become knowledgeable on a coaching basis rather than on a "spy and punish" basis. We have too often tried to solve problems by putting in a new person rather than evaluating skill deficiencies and providing education or therapy to correct them.

Dehumanization and Lack of Opportunity for Self-Affirmation

From a study of 10 organizations, Chris Argyris concluded that executives represent a more potent source of dehumanization, conformity, and ineffective decision making than does computer technology: "The biggest single contributor to the dehumanization of the decision-making process was the way the executives dealt with each other and the kinds of group dynamics they created. Interdepartmental rivalry tends to reward the mediocre men but discourages first-class executives."[20]

Sometimes we can learn a great deal from negative examples.

For instance, the so-called brainwashing effort by the Chinese during the Korean War, in which wide use was made of a number of variables which, taken together, were relatively effective in reducing motivation and encouraging apathy and psychological failure. This state was induced by the Chinese in order to better control the men for whom they were responsible.

Apathy was brought about through the *creation of an ambiguous situation where opportunities for self-affirmation from significant others were virtually nonexistent.* Warm understanding letters were censored while critical, harping, or "Dear John" letters were delivered. This blocked opportunities for self-affirmation and emotional support from family. The creation of self-criticism groups by the Chinese and an effective informing system cut the individuals off from self-affirmation and emotional support from their peer group. That this was ostensibly done with a certain amount of kindness left nowhere for frustration and hostility to be discharged, except back against the individual. The ultimate in hostility towards oneself is, of course, some form of suicide.

How is the Chinese control of a prisoner-of-war camp relevant to the young engineers and scientists committing professional suicide in a big American corporation? Can our understanding of these dynamics from Korea explain what happens to the "organization man"? We have seen how under Theory X and the theories of Scientific Management the task was all-important. Its performance was clearly specified, and relatively little attention was paid to individuals' emotional integrity. They could feel what they wanted to, and what they felt was usually some anger and resentment against the organization. This was freely expressed within the peer group—even encouraged. The task and the feelings were left separate.

Under the human relations philosophy, the feelings of the employee were wooed with considerable success. But under the individual commitment philosophy that evolved later, the individual's feelings were expected, almost as a condition of employment, to be involved in the task and positive. Sometimes it was expressed with kindness and sometimes with brutal frankness; but in most situations managers expected the involvement of employees' feelings in the task. This began an era in which the control of one's own feelings and the feelings of others became an integral part of the job. It led to the denial of the self and the loss of emotional integrity. The results of this are only gradually being realized. When individuals allow external forces to dictate what they will feel, the scene is set for self-alienation and cultural anomie. Professional suicide is the logical result of the strains produced by this kind of environment, with its conflict between Cultural values stressing aggressiveness, individual accomplishment, and change and interpersonal relationships Stressing helpfulness to others while accepting no help for oneself. Self-esteem rests on coming to grips with problems (without upsetting continual advancement), but the ambiguous situation makes this impossible.

Organizations and entrenched groups of people have ways of frustrating bright, young, aggressive individuals interested in change and of withholding the top-level support so necessary to maintain their interest and motivation for any length of time. There are many ways of dealing with deviant members of the ingroup, of converting human beings into exploitable resources or of reshaping their egos and social identifications as persons to make them fit transformed social arrangements, or of removing those who cannot be made to fit these transformations. Killing or avoidance of contact (alternative modes for doing the same kinds of things) become less adequate for coping with persons outside normal ingroup modes of interaction. Treatment, by interrupting the self-destructive process, makes it hard to analyze. As hostility is focused away from the self to the very real problems in the environment (if at not too high a level) the individual usually leaves.

The Lack of Evaluation and Criticism

We have found that people who develop high self-esteem gauge their individual worth primarily by their achievements and their treatment within their own interpersonal environment rather than by the more general and abstract norms of success, such as physical attractiveness, or family social position. The parents of children with high self-esteem indicated that they placed greater value on their children's achievement of excellence than on their adjustment or accommodation to other persons. They established definite standards of performance for their children, which enabled them to know whether or not they had succeeded at a task, how far they had fallen short if they had failed, and what efforts would be needed to be successful.

The development of independence and self-reliance is fostered by a well-structured, demanding environment, rather than by nearly unlimited permissiveness and the freedom to explore in an unfocused way (characteristic of management by subordinate commitment).

A major symptom of mental illness in our times is disorientation.[21] This is characteristic of professional suicides. A business organization without some type of "performance review" feedback in the formal system, which establishes a highly competitive atmosphere among employees in the informal system, can expect a good deal of non-goal-related activity. A philosophy of management that does not orient but accepts as a major premise its inability to accurately define organizational purpose and direction, contributes relatively little to the effective use of its human resources.

There was a commonly accepted, widely prevailing standard in the organization being studied against giving performance reviews. Managers said, "We do not believe in reviewing an individual's performance only once or twice a year; we believe it should be done daily." Subordinates agreed that managers did comment on the various aspects of their work, but all wanted some evaluation of their total performance on an official basis, in contrast to the informal inputs which change from day to day depending on mood.

An organizationally accepted excuse for not giving performance reviews is that subordinates do not want them. This is never checked out directly, by either the boss or the personnel department, and becomes a screen behind which managers can hide their unwillingness to give reviews (and their lack of competence in being open about what they want). Human effectiveness, however, is not just a subordinate problem, but a problem of team (leader-subordinate, subordinate-peer, leader-peer, leader-leader) effectiveness. The lack of feedback and formal evaluations of performance make it very difficult for those individuals interested in working on organizational goals to do so effectively.

The retention of highly creative, highly capable people in menial and organizationally irrelevant jobs appears to be sometimes used as proof of how bright the boss is: "Look who I have reporting to me." Because there are no performance reviews, no one really knows how good the individual is. As a result, some may find it reassuring to see an individual who has been highly creative in the past relegated to some menial task: "Every time I look at him, I have confirmation of how much more successful I am than he."

In situations of uncertainty, people need to compare themselves with others, not only for the purpose of self-evaluation, but also to gauge how they are going to approach tasks. They have to evaluate their strategies and the strategies other people are using, and they have to consider how to change their strategies to handle the task more adequately. According to the "social comparison theory," uncertainty about one's ability can lead to competitiveness for the purpose of obtaining a more accurate evaluation of one's own ability.

Persons who do not know where they stand in their abilities or on a personality-attractiveness scale can be expected to have serious difficulty in setting their levels of aspiration and in understanding their competence for tasks requiring certain levels of ability.[22] Some jobs they will be able to do and some not; sometimes the job will be beneath their capabilities, and only occasionally will they hit it just right. Obviously, individuals in this situation will sooner or later experience some form of social punishment. The anticipation of such consequences will be sufficient to generate stress.

Not knowing if one is able to pursue one's interests in a satisfying or profitable way produces additional stress. But even if individuals live in an environment where accurate evaluation and utilization of their abilities are important, there will be some stress generated by the unknown evaluation of certain nonpublic abilities. To the extent that self-evaluation uncertainties can be reduced, individuals are relieved of stress. And stress increases to the extent that making accurate comparisons is difficult.

Individuals whose performance cannot be or is not evaluated

by objective criteria will use the performance of others as a standard of measurement. Specifically, they will try to raise or lower their performance so that it is close to the performance of others whom they regard as reflecting a relevant standard.[23] Knowledge of results typically achieves better performance than ignorance of results.[24] At least some of this effect may be attributed to the interest, attention, and avoidance of boredom that knowledge of results can provide.

Big organizations encourage the use of subtle deprivations.[25] Individuals may not know for some time that they have been disciplined and the actual reasons may elude them permanently. Peers will tell you what you did wrong, but no one will tell you what you did right.

The Stress of Anxiety as a Motivator (Motivation by Crisis)

Because management in our study no longer really understood the nature of its business, it became anxious, and this anxiety was inevitably transmitted downward. In place of using meaningful organizational goals as motivators, management had to find other means to motivate workers. One way of motivating people is through anxiety. It seemed to have almost become policy never to solve a problem until it became a crisis, perhaps because it was found that people will work harder (but, of course, less creatively) to resolve a crisis than to solve a routine problem. Lacking organizational goals and directions, management provided push and motivation through the creation of crises and the production of anxiety states as a means of promoting activity.

One of the ways for an organization or a boss to appear highly productive is to imply over and over again in many ways, "You are not doing well enough," "Look at all the problems." Or, more benignly, "Look at all the challenges there are for you here." This generates an air of anxiety and frantic behavioral activity that eventually permeates the atmosphere and results in people looking busy, but usually has a negative effect on creative kinds of activity. People do not think most creatively under prolonged pressure. However, it is one way of getting activity for a time from those who have lived under constant pressure for so long and have become so fatigued that only under the pressure of a crisis can they respond at all.

When organizational goals are not defined, the individual's roles and the roles and power positions of others are not defined, the result is that the individual is left feeling perplexed and anxious. The implication of management by subordinate commitment is that subordinates must set their own goals because organizational goals are nonexistent or kept hidden. This (in Durkheim's terms) allows the subordinate's egoism full rein, and tremendous amounts of anxiety are created.

Cattrell and Scheir found that there are not many kinds of anxiety (healthy and unhealthy) but only one, and that when it is present it is usually a symptom of a disease, such as neurosis, depression, or schizophrenia.[26] Inducing a state of anxiety is one of the chief means of breaking people down and is used extensively to accomplish thought control. They found that anxiety "is the opposite of a motivational drive. It has a disruptive influence on the mind. It either disorganizes or is a symptom of disorganization."[27]

The symptoms of anxiety are lack of confidence; the sense of guilt and worthlessness; unwillingness to venture; dependency; readiness to become fatigued, irritable and discouraged; uncertainty about oneself; suspicion of others; and general tenseness.

> If you shake the surface on which a snail is resting, it withdraws into its shell. If you shake it repeatedly, the snail after a while fails to react. In the same way, a sea anemone which is disturbed by a drop of water falling on the water surface above it ceases to be disturbed if drops continue falling. A bird stops flying away from a rustling motion if the motion is steadily repeated. Most organisms stop responding to a stimulus repeated over and over again (unless the response is reinforced by reward or avoidance of punishment).[28]

Another method for motivating by anxiety is to view start-up costs on a new contract as end-of-the-month losses—as though there could be anything but a loss at the end of the month on a new contract. The result is that everyone becomes very anxious, works long hours, becomes fatigued, gets panicky, and makes poor decisions. Then people get replaced and things slowly become more profitable, but mostly because the start-up costs have by now been paid.

A common antidote for anxiety is activity. Although anxiety generates a great deal of activity, it is usually at a low creative level. Under conditions of anxiety, the higher centers of the brain do not come into use. The individual runs and runs fast, but the work produced is of relatively low quality. As anxiety mounts, the individual spends more and more time in motor activity in an effort to reduce anxiety and less and less time on mental and planning activities. (This is commonly known as "dazzling them with footwork.")

The Dutch zoologist, N. Tinbergen, coined the term "displacement behavior" to describe substitute behavior that appears to have little meaning. When a situation becomes too stressful, displacement activity may serve as an escape hatch from the emotional impact of the frustrating circumstances. G. V. Hamilton in *Objective Psychopathology* describes the reactions of animals (and human beings) subject to an unsolvable problem: sheep appear to nibble, goats unaccountably look over the walls, cats wash themselves.

Because of the anxiety in the system, there is a tendency to go with short-range, expedient decisions and solutions rather than searching further for creative decisions and solutions. In an organization engaged in the mass production of standard parts, where quality is relatively unimportant, it may be effective to maintain a high level of anxiety under which people move rapidly with relatively little thought. In the mass production of simple parts, anxiety has the effect of making people work harder and may be functional. While its effect on people is to make them work faster, they neglect to plan, so make more mistakes. In complex systems, this can be very costly indeed. An error that reduces a simple 5-dollar valve to scrap is obviously less costly than an error that reduces a complex 60,000-dollar nozzle to scrap.

It is also important to note that the long hours of overtime generated by this method of motivating have a destructive effect on family relationships and home life. A sense of total commitment to the organization and the lack of any clear boundaries for what is expected, plus the anxiety generated by too much to do and not enough time to do it, appears to cause people to run harder and harder and to become more and more emotionally fatigued, until eventually they begin to develop the symptoms of professional suicide. Those who can leave impossible situations do leave; while those who cannot because of family situations or personal commitment eventually develop into suicides.

In addition to the anxiety created by managers who feel this is a good way to motivate workers, anxiety is generated internally by the fear of not doing a good enough job, not being accepted and appreciated, and the lack of a sense of accomplishment. Anxiety is fostered by unrealistic expectations, the lack of a sense of purpose, and the lack of a goal orientation to life.

The Stress of Competition as a Motivator

Competition and hard bargaining as a means of motivation toward organizational objectives bring about a number of stresses and undesirable consequences.[29, 30,] * Before using these methods, the following questions should be considered:

1.   What happens *within* competing groups when competition is used to motivate?

   a.   Each group or individual pulls in close and sees others as enemies.

   b.   Loyalty increases: willingness to help others decreases.

   c.   Each sees only the best in itself and the worst others; each puts up a filter or a screen to protect this projection.

   d.   Members close ranks—increasing feelings that "we are good; others are bad."

   e.   The group demands more conformity from its members, and less individuality and creativity are allowed.

   f.   Leadership changes; autocracy becomes acceptable.

   g.   Group atmosphere changes from relaxed, unhurried, in-depth consideration of problems to more frantic, superfi-

*Reproduced by special permission from *Human Relations Training News*, "Some Dynamics of Intergroup Competition," by Jerry Harvey, vol. 8, nos. 3 and 4, pp. 1–4, 1964–65, NTL Institute for Applied Behavioral Science.

cial efforts; from high maintenance of interpersonal relationships to low.

h.   The group becomes more structured; subgroups may form but discord is kept hidden, visible only to the ingroup.

2.   What happens *between* competing groups or individuals when competition is used to motivate?

a.   Inaccurate and uncomplimentary stereotypes form.

b.   Members become hostile toward others.

c.   Interaction and communication decrease.

d.   Members do not listen to adversaries but hear only that which supports their own position.

3.   What happens to the bosses who eventually must judge the competition they have arranged?

a.   Unconsciously aware of the consequences of judging, they try to postpone announcing the winners in the hopes of making all groups and individuals feel successful, but postponing does not usually have this result.

b.   They find that they cannot divorce themselves from the situation and be truly neutral, which makes some participants in the competition feel cheated.

c.   They feel tremendous conflict between loyalty to the groups and the judge's role.

4.   What happens to the winners of the competition?

a.   They become trapped in the rigid structure that won for them.

b.   They retain their cohesion and are even more cohesive.

c.   They find that questioning the situation that produced victory is psychologically impossible.

d.   They become "fat and happy."

e.   Tension is released; no more fighting spirit.

f.   More play develops—and complacency.

g.   There is high cooperation but little work.

5.   What happens to the losers of the competition?

a.   First, they deny the reality of losing and continue to rationalize that their solution was really better.

b.   Next, they concern themselves with how to win next time, even if there is not going to be a next time.

c.   Finally, they tend to splinter and start a scapegoating process.

d.   Fights develop and reorganizations occur.

e.   Tension increases; they ready themselves to dig harder.

f.   Leaders and the organization are blamed.

g.   They may learn a lot about themselves.

6.   What happens to chronically defeated groups?

a.   They tend to divide into subgroups with both cliques and social isolates.

b.   There is mutual disparagement between cliques. Rumor is abundant, especially gloomy rumor.

c.   Some members quit and these are usually then considered "good ones." The group develops a "servant self-image," stops initiating ideas, squashes innovators, and does only what it is sure superiors want.

d.   They see themselves as weak competitors and others as powerful, against whom they cannot hope to win.

e.   As they come to feel less and less valued, their capacity to respond adequately deteriorates.

f.   The self-image of defeat leads to inappropriate activities and inactivity which reconfirms over and over their low estimate of themselves.

g.   Halting or correcting this unhealthy state of affairs usually requires active intervention from outside the group.

7.   What happens to the group leaders?

a.   They experience conflict between their own strategies and the mandate given them by the group.

b.   They experience severe tension resulting from being responsible for the group's success or failure.

The win-lose feelings continue to exist long after the problem is over. Feelings of conflict may never be completely resolved, which makes it very difficult to establish future more collaborative relationships. Competition as a motivator does not achieve the results that are most organizationally useful for continuing effectiveness. Instead of using a competition model to accomplish organizational tasks, effective managers will increasingly want to make greater use of collaborative models.

In competitive situations, the element of surprise is an advantage and trust is a disadvantage. It is thus no surprise that individual competition is a powerful motivator and can be successful in environments where individual effort is organizationally relevant (such as sales). However, in environments where successful efforts cannot be accomplished by one person alone, a climate based on individual competition is nonfunctional.

A system based on individual competitiveness not only destroys collaborative efforts but removes talented people from the organization. The introduction of a well-trained person into a position traditionally requiring less training creates problems. People with more seniority but less training become concerned that the route to advancement, which used to be longevity, may be changing in favor of education or performance. Peers with greater seniority but less education feel threatened by the new employee. It is difficult for the intellectual "rate buster" not to have to compete with peers who see no advantage for them in the new person's presence.

The organization needs highly educated, dedicated people if it is to advance, but these people often lose out in the long run when placed in competitive situations with the bureaucrats. If there are four committed persons in a group and one who is not, the one who is not can bargain with the others and usually come out on top. People who are committed and dedicated have difficulty in bargaining. A management philosophy of subordinate commitment and a philosophy of doing on your own what needs to be done may seduce overcommitted people into doing self-destructive things.

A good deal of stress is generated in competitive environments when the individual engenders hostility and rejection in others— which would normally cause him to attenuate his competitiveness except that the demands made by others (sometimes the very same others) keep him in the battle.

In competitive situations personal success frequently means someone else will fail. In some people with humanitarian instincts, there may be an unconscious fear of success because this means that someone else will not succeed, and they would rather fail themselves than cause this hardship for another.

People reared in deprived settings—a "jungle" environment—quickly learn how to protect themselves and how to fight to get their needs met. Many from the American middle class have been reared in environments where it was not necessary to fight for survival and they did not have to compete viciously to get their needs met. Their psychological needs, their security needs, their belonging needs, even their recognition needs were met by their affluent, benign environments. As a result, these people are highly "other-oriented." They are concerned with making the world a better place; and it is these people who go into professions and into organizations to improve them. When asked to commit themselves to improving the organization, they did so, assuming that the organization would show its appreciation by providing them with the information, the support, the resources, and the authority to do the job. Sometimes it did, but often it did not. The growing awareness that the organization was not really interested in meeting their needs and the severe frustration that resulted from being assigned an impossible or an unimportant task precipitated suicide symptomatology.

From studies of cooperation/competition in prison camps, we learn that when individuals can get what they want by cooperating, they will cooperate. But when resources are kept in such short supply that everyone cannot get what they want, individuals will compete. An aspect of the organizational climate is hard bargaining with subordinates—a philosophy of "give them less than they need, and this will increase organizational effectiveness."

Pepitone points out that the usual stress in the junior level of an organization comes from the severe competition at that level—junior executives are almost entirely evaluated against each other for promotions and other special rewards.[31] Top managers, on the other hand, are evaluated against ideal or quasi-absolute standards. Also, at the top there are more dimensions of evaluation, and a more complex set of considerations is involved in the reward system. Because the junior positions are relatively unattractive, stronger self-improvement tendencies are found in the junior ranks. The magnitude of stress at a given level in the hierarchy is inversely related to the mobility from that to the next higher level. (One way management sought to deal with such stress was to deny that such levels exist.)

Social comparisons in natural situations can be an important source of stress. In such circumstances it cannot be assumed that people will change their evaluations so that they do not compare themselves with those far more capable. Mechanic found, in a study of doctoral students, that instead of deciding not to compare themselves with other persons or to leave the situation, individuals who compare themselves with others more capable get very anxious and upset, and do not function very well for a few days. Then they start to avoid the persons who stimulate the comparison and their anxiety.[32] We saw the same response in the business community.

The negative side of individual competitiveness can be counteracted through the establishment of group goals and group grading systems. In the well-known study by Deutsch undergraduates in a human relations course were divided into two groups and asked to solve intellectual and human relations problems. One group worked competitively; members were ranked according to how well they did on the problems *as individuals.* In the other group, the class worked the problem as a whole and was ranked *in relation to other classes.* In this second group, each individual received the same rank as the class. As could be expected, students in the competitive group showed less coordination of effort, greater redundancy of role behavior, lower volume of communication with one another, and less interpersonal liking.[33]

The Stress of Guilt as a Motivator

Socialized people, people who care, experience guilt when their behavior or their feelings conflict with the demands of the value system they have adopted or when they have not fulfilled some of the expectations held by themselves or by others. Obviously, some people make stronger demands (expect more of themselves) than others. These people consequently experience sharper conflicts and are thus more guilt prone than others.

Schein defined five kinds of guilt:

1. Social Guilt: the recognition that much of what one has in life has not been earned, but has been given by accident of birth.

2. Ego or Identity Guilt: the recognition of failure to live up to one's image of oneself.

3. Personal Guilt: the feeling that comes from wearing a mask; the discovery or recognition of having deliberately or involuntarily deceived another person about oneself.

4. Loyalty Guilt: the recognition that one has failed in service to a group with which one is strongly identified, or has violated its norms, or defiled its image by behaving in a manner not consistent with what is expected of members of that group.

5. Situational Guilt: guilt aroused by the magnification by others of minor infractions or petty acts that normally do not run counter to the individual's basic values or self-image, particularly when they are perceived as having been stimulated by great stress. Such feelings of guilt indicate that the individual is beginning to accept some of the norms of the conflicting value system.[34]

Guilt can be used as a motivator and some managers make excellent use of it. A study by Adams found that unqualified people who were overpaid tended to work extremely hard to justify what they were paid. This was interpreted as a desire to vindicate themselves or to raise their worth in the eyes of the employer.[35]

Among prisoners in Communist Chinese prison camps, guilt was found to be one of the central forces motivating prisoners to change.[36] "Recently, as a result of the study of data from Chinese Communist prisons, more attention has been given to *social* isolation, a state in which the subject may be in the midst of others but feels himself completely isolated from them. The effects of such a condition are at present only reportable anecdotally, there being little theory and less experimental data available to throw light on them."[37]

Early in their careers many of the people who developed into professional suicides felt that "after all the freedom the organization has given me and after all the confidence that has been expressed in me, how can I work less than 60 hours a week?"

Employees are told that the ability to do a job is not just a test of one's ability as a worker, but also of one's worth as a person.

If the project is then not successful, dignity and self-worth as an individual is under question. If a project fails, it becomes extremely difficult for some people to look elsewhere for work: "If I could not succeed in this setting where everyone has been so nice, how can I possibly succeed anywhere else?" A powerful means for holding people in the organization is the sense of guilt engendered by the feeling that "I have not done a good enough job and I must remain until I succeed."

The Problem of Incrementalism

If you think of a game that involves moving pieces over a board, where players move in turn, each moving one piece one square at a time, you will notice the game proceeds at a slow tempo by small increments. The situation on the board may change character in the course of the play, but it does so by a succession of small changes that can be observed, appreciated, and adapted to. There is plenty of time for the mistakes of individual players, or mutual mistakes that destroy value for both, to be observed, adapted to, and avoided in subsequent play. If there is communication, there is time for the players to bargain and to avoid moves that involve mutual destruction.

Suppose, however, that instead the pieces can be moved several at a time in any direction and any distance and that the rules make the outcome of any hostile clash enormously destructive for one or both sides. Now the game is not so incremental. Things can happen abruptly. There may be a temptation to surprise attack. While one can see what the situation is at a particular moment, one cannot project it more than a move or two ahead. There is less chance to develop a modus vivendi, or a tradition of trust, or dominant and submissive roles. The pace of the game brings things to a head before much experience has been gained or much of an understanding has been reached.[38]

Just as advances in technology have vastly changed the way in which international politics are played, so have advances in technology changed the ways in which the business game is played. No longer can the manager manage by making minor adjustments at a slow rate. Faced with sweeping problems, he must be

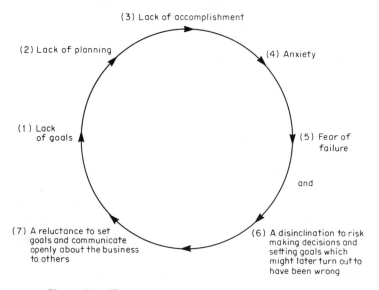

Figure 5-1   The vicious cycle of organizational deterioration.

prepared to make sweeping changes. And, he must be continually looking over his shoulder to see what is gaining on him. All of this creates tremendous challenge and opportunity. But, it can also generate anxiety and apprehension and stress.

The Vicious Cycle of Organizational and Employee Deterioration

Lack of goals leads to lack of planning. Lack of planning leads to lack of accomplishment. Lack of accomplishment leads to anxiety and fear of failure. Anxiety breeds reluctance to risk making decisions and setting goals which might later turn out to have been wrong. Fear of failure results in reluctance to set goals and to communicate openly about the business. Reluctance to set goals and communicate openly leads back to the lack of goal setting and planning. And the vicious cycle repeats itself (see Figure 5-1). As one manager said, "The thing that really grinds you up is having so many things that you cannot correct."

Miscellaneous Organizational Characteristics
Contributing to Professional Suicide

In addition to the organizational characteristics already mentioned as having an influence on the development of professional suicide, there are a number of others, including:

The whittle down process

"Nickel and diming" a guy to death

The "first guy rarely succeeds" syndrome

The stretch syndrome

The runaway generator effect

The concept of commitment

The law of human relativity

The king of the hill concept

The lack of manager development and training

The boss as therapist

Management by ground swell

A value system based on end-of-the-month profit dollars

Management by myopia

The legitimation of the predator

Being left alone by the boss as a reward

The high value placed on optimism

The Rasputin maneuver

The Dale Carnegie maneuver

The lack of channels for getting things done

Organization as big brother

The development of recognition hunger

The lack of succession planning and avoidance of the crown prince syndrome

Chaining people to the organization

The lack of a boss who cares

An orientation of short-term survival instead of growth; the lack of interpersonal competence

The Whittle Down Process.   This refers to the management practice of always giving good people less than they really need to do a job. There is a frequently heard remark. "If you gave everyone all they asked for, you could never make a profit," and, "If you had all the resources you needed, anyone could do it. The test of your skill is to see how few resources you can use and still get the job done." However, when projects fail for lack of sufficient resources, subordinates are accused of not being managerially competent enough to get what they really need.

The old-timers recognize this practice, but the conscientious, sincere young ones are frustrated and often "killed" by not getting enough resources to do the required job. After a time, workers get the impression that they will receive just enough support to keep them from quitting but not enough to enable them to do a really good job. As a result, they soon begin to feel that management is not really interested in their doing a good job. The management point of view is that a person can always get by with just a little bit less.

"Nickel and Diming a Guy to Death." This refers to the tendency of some bosses to load a subordinate with so many picayune details of a minor but immediate nature that little time is left for the employee's major job or for being creative at it. This technique is frequently used by bosses who feel threatened by a subordinate. The subordinate is kept busy with trivia in order not to be available for jobs of greater organizational significance and visibility. It is also used by frightened bosses who burden their subordinates with negative defensive duties so that a major portion of their time is spent in nonproductive ways. This point of view is characterized by the efficiency expert's philosophy that a person can always do just a little bit more.

The First Guy on a Project Rarely Succeeds. This commonly heard organizational adage is partly a result of inadequate definition of the project and what is needed to complete it successfully, and partly a result of hard bargaining by bosses who do not understand the technical problems. As a result, the project manager rarely gets enough to do the job right. Not until the project fails does management realize that the resources allocated were inadequate. Inevitably, the second person on the project gets more support than the first; and the first never knows if the job might not have been successful the first time with the additional support the second person received. "We do not have time to do it right, but we always have time to do it over" (usually, however, with a new manager).

The desire to keep the organization "lean" and to always give less than what is asked for is viewed positively by most managers because it maintains anxiety at a high level. It makes people extend themselves and it heightens competition, all of which makes the organization appear dedicated and hard-working.

The Stretch Syndrome. This refers to the way some bosses tax their subordinates by setting goals beyond those that the subordinates feel they can achieve. If the subordinates reach these larger goals, then the next time even greater goals are set. This often goes on until the subordinates get tired of being stretched and develop some form of professional suicide. As when a juggler who is asked to keep two balls in the air and then three and then four finally overreaches, it is not just the most recently added ball that falls, but all of them.

The Runaway Generator Effect. This effect is commonly seen among managers who have lived under prolonged and too heavy loads only to be relieved of all responsibility and suddenly placed in staff jobs. Having labored under a heavy load and then being reduced to almost no load results in a response commonly seen in machinery that has been subjected to a heavy load and is then suddenly relieved. There is a brief sense of relief, but then comes the question of what to do with the unused energy. Resourceful people may find things to keep them busy; others may "spin apart." People known to be under stress are sometimes sent on vacations (that is, periods of enforced idleness). With problems back at the shop that they know have to be solved, this common management ploy is not often seen by subordinates as helpful.

The Concept of "Commitment." The idea of being "committed" is widely used within the organization. This means that individuals are dedicated to the performance of tasks which they will exert every effort to accomplish regardless of personal inconvenience and broader organizational needs.

In animal experiments the pigeon who persists in a task despite the absence of payoff is "stubborn" or "stupid" (the snarl words), or he has "character" (the purr word for the same data).[39] Indeed, when a person persists in a task despite frustration and despite defeats, we say "He doesn't know when he's been licked," or "He has character." It all depends on our relationship with that person.

A philosophy of commitment means that each employee personally assumes the responsibility for improving the organization. Because this task is too great for individuals acting alone (without leadership, without an overall plan based on realistic goals, without adequate support) they frequently fail. A philosophy of management by subordinate commitment and of doing on one's own what needs to be done frequently seduces overcommitted people into doing things that are self-destructive and organizationally destructive.

The Law of Human Relativity. This law says, "To the extent that I diminish you, relatively I advance."[40] The extent to which outside competition is absent is the extent to which a company can tolerate widespread internal incompetence without becoming seriously concerned. If I can see that no one is capable of doing my job, my survival chances appear strengthened.

The King of the Hill Concept. This is a children's game that is also played in business. When a need is recognized in the organization, resources move quickly toward meeting this need; but lack of coordination and inadequate role definition lead to confusion in trying to meet the need. As a result, some compete vigorously and some withdraw, but the decision about who does what is frequently based on individual personality characteristics rather than rationally based on whose skills are most appropriate. For a rational decision to be made, there must be either a boss (Theory X) or a team (participative management). A philosophy of management by default and the assumption that people can act effectively all on their own is not realistic, according to the observations in the organization studied.

The Lack of Manager Development and Training. This is encouraged by a philosophy of "Throw them in and see if they sink" and "The cream rises to the top." (One manager pointed out, "So does the scum.") A "learn as you make mistakes" approach to manager development creates many problems for young managers and for the organization. For many, it results in failure experiences, which, if not adequately analyzed, can profoundly affect their professional futures.

A child who has been taught to swim by being thrown into deep water, pulled out on going under, and then dunked again may learn to swim as well as a child who has been gradually introduced to water through more benign swimming instruction procedures. But children taught by the former method, as distinguished from a more gradual approach, are likely to have very different responses to swimming and to the instruction of others. It is also very expensive for the organization to have young managers learning their trade through experimenting with real people and with real dollars, when the learning would be better and much less costly for the organization if training could take place off the job with simulated dollars.

The Boss as Therapist. Some bosses enjoy the sense of power over dependent people. As a result, they unconsciously surround themselves with weak people and drive out the competent by not giving any attention.

Management by Ground Swell. Decisions are delayed until they are made by circumstances. There appear to be fewer repercussions from wrong decisions if they were forced upon management by fate.

A Value System Based on End-of-the-Month Profit Dollars. This value system tends to be ends-oriented without anyone overseeing the means. One way to maximize the end-of-the-month profit dollars (over the short run) is to make no investment in the future or, more drastically, to begin a gradual liquidation of the business. A climate that emphasizes end-of-the-month profit dollars with little apparent awareness of the investment that must be made for future business and growth is debilitating to the organization and the people in it.

Management by Myopia. Very similarly, bosses who think their reputations are made on a month-to-month basis operate so as to maximize end-of-the-month profits. Because of this, managers under these bosses may lose sight of the future. Middle managers are not given enough time to develop future talent. One manager is quoted as saying about a long-range development effort, "I am not interested in building a future for someone else."

The Legitimation of the Predator. Without goals and without leadership, a method of accomplishment was instituted which might be called "opportunities for self-actualization," but can also be known as "the legitimation of the predator." When an organization has grown very rapidly or when the technology of a business has changed abruptly, it frequently leads to management by crisis. This is usually a sign that those in managerial control are not sure where the organization is going and do not have a realistic business plan. Unable to direct the business themselves, they assign the responsibility for organizational planning and direction to subordinates, with the rationale that this will be a good experience for youthful subordinates. Management by crisis is also called opportunistic management, and while it may yield short-run gains, it usually results in a net loss in the long run.

The reason for this is that with no one acting as "company overseer" each department (as well as individuals) eventually learns that it is foolish to expect fair treatment.[41] This leads to an everyone-for-himself, every-department-for-itself reaction. Soon everyone is thinking exclusively in terms of personal needs. The fences go up and the games start being played. Divisive struggles start between and within departments. People stop showing any appreciation for the problems of others. Rumors are used as tactical weapons, and the lack of good human relations becomes increasingly obvious. The result is that with so much time and effort going into interpersonal and interdepartmental warfare, little time is left over for doing productive work.

The way to avoid suicide is to be aware of the reality in which you find yourself. If the organization encourages self-actualization, and there are few rewards for people other than the joys they themselves can extract from the moment, then it is important to know this, and it should influence where you spend your time and exert your energies.

Being Left Alone by the Boss as a Reward. There is a rather common saying among bosses, "If I leave you alone, you must know you are doing all right." Unfortunately, subordinates do not always look at it this way. If failure is the only way of being noticed, then many human beings may find themselves setting up the conditions for failure. A study by Nathan H. Azrin found that when a pigeon was shocked every time it pecked, pecking increased, and when punishment was absent, pecking stopped. This behavior sounds very masochistic unless you know that even though a shock followed each response, food was also sometimes given. If undergoing punishment is the only way to obtain food or recognition, then animals (and human beings) may submit to, or even set up, conditions for punishment![42]

The High Value Placed on Optimism. When the organization and the decisions of higher management are always viewed optimistically, it is difficult to change. Change requires a great deal of effort, and the view that things are really not so bad frequently paralyzes people doing something about a system that is gradually deteriorating.

The Rasputin Maneuver. You gain control over the communication network by telling the boss you will handle whatever is in question, or that it is not important enough for him. Feed him information that is favorable to you or for things you want, and block information that is not favorable to you. If he allows you to do this long enough, you can have him under complete control.

The Dale Carnegie Maneuver. You "get in the guy's guts" and then hold the relationship as collateral for his doing what you want. This is an excellent maneuver by which the self-actualizers can subvert the organization's resources to their own ends (noble as these may be).

The Lack of Channels for Getting Things Done. The lack of policy, and the lack of established routine for dealing with frequently recurring problems is a severe handicap to those trying to work within the organization. In the company studied, in an effort to free people from administrative bureaucracy and red tape, line charts were hidden and the formal channels for getting things done were kept vague. No one was ever completely sure who was directing subsections of the organization. The best way to get an issue resolved seemed to be to find a champion who would, on a personal basis, promote it with top management. An example of this occurred when expensive electric typewriters were given to highly paid secretaries who did little actual typing and denied to production typists working on proposals. There were no methods for correcting this decision other than a personal plea. And this earned black marks for the person who championed the cause.

There appeared to be no formal channels for getting the organization to act, only informal channels. Such organizations tend to function as one vast political system. The extent to which policy can be formulated and procedures routinized is the extent to which valuable time can be spent in other ways than on applying political pressure or continually "reinventing the wheel."

The Organization as Big Brother. There was a tendency for the organization to turn any complaints or criticisms back on the individual, always maintaining that the organization is right in whatever it does and that any individual who feels put upon has no real right to feel that way. Any lack of organizational accomplishment is always the subordinate's fault, even though it was the boss who denied the information, the time, and the resources.

The boss wanted people who said they could do what needed to be done, but without objective records kept on what they had done before. Personnel records on prior accomplishments were not kept. The important assignments frequently went to those not familiar with the problems. Because the more informed were aware of the problems, they were frequently bypassed for those less informed but more enthusiastic. Past competence and technical knowledge of the subject seemed less important in assigning projects than loyalty, commitment and enthusiasm.

The Development of Recognition Hunger. This is the feeling of not being appreciated that comes from doing a good job over extended periods without any praise or pats on the back. The lack of recognition and appreciation for hardworking employees appears to be the result of:

1. A highly competitive atmosphere where those who get recognition are likely to be moved up the ladder past you

2. An anxiety-provoking, crisis-oriented environment where there is no time for anything but working on pressing problems

3. The lack of manager development and interpersonal competence. Many managers know how to criticize and work problem situations, but do not know how to give recognition and appreciation

It is thought by many managers that expressing appreciation for a good job well done stimulates requests for salary increases.

"If you appreciate my work, don't give me words; put it in my pay envelope," is a commonly heard comment of hourly personnel. In a highly mobile, fast-moving industry it is difficult to know just how much to pay people; and, of course, salary dollars detract from end-of-the-month dollar profits. The fear of stimulating requests for salary increases seems to be an additional reason for withholding recognition.

The Lack of Succession Planning and Avoidance of the Crown Prince Syndrome. There is recognition of the immense power that rests in the hands of the peer group. Experience has apparently shown that anyone recognized as the successor to the boss immediately loses cooperation from peers. The emphasis on individual competition appears to severely limit the amount of help peers will give to anyone obviously in line for the boss's job. As a result, management tends to cloak its evaluation of people and its plan for people's futures. The result of this is recognition hunger in subordinates and lack of organizational workforce and succession planning.

Chaining People to the Organization. The lack of any retirement benefits for less than 10 years of service is a reason given by some people for remaining in the organization after they might otherwise have left. The presence of people who are "just putting in time" and the reluctance of managers to confront a situation thought to be so potentially damaging to the employee, results in costs to the organization which may be well in excess of what would be incurred by establishing an earlier date for the vesting of retirement benefits. Certain other company policies that are time dependent (such as stock savings plans) also result in inhibiting the flow of people between companies.

The Lack of a Boss Who Cares. The boss may be too busy working on personal goals either within or outside the organization to care about subordinates. This is very upsetting to the bright aggressive people who want to accomplish something. A few noncaring or preoccupied managers scattered throughout the organization can have a very depressing effect on the organization's climate.

An Orientation of Short-Term Survival Instead of Growth. A major cause of professional suicide in both individuals and organizations is the establishment of various prac-

Table 5-4 Two Kinds of Organizational Philosophies

A Survival-Oriented Philosophy	A Growth-Oriented Philosophy
(Characteristic of a defensive organization concerned with survival and not making mistakes, essentially management by control)	(Characteristic of an aggressive organization concerned with growth and making a contribution, essentially participative management by objectives)

Communications

Communication of information is restricted because people cannot be trusted to be careful enough with it.	Information is shared widely because people can be trusted, and they need information in order to do good work.
Knowledge of the organization is power and must be tightly controlled by insecure people.	Knowledge is power and should be widely shared if people are to do their best.
If you communicate, you show your ignorance.	If you communicate, you learn something.

Goal Setting

Encourage subordinates to set goals, but do not set any yourself—thus you can hold them accountable if they do not reach their goals, but you will not be accountable.	Set goals yourself and encourage your people to set goals—thus all can work together toward common goals and a common purpose.
Keep charters vague—thus any mistakes can be laid at someone else's door, and you can assume credit for those things that go well.	Make charters as precise as possible—in this way people are most clear on what they should be doing and can channel their energies accordingly.
Pass responsibility either downward or upward—if things do not happen or they go wrong, someone else is to blame.	Take responsibility—when things go right, you can legitimately take credit. When things go wrong, you learn from experience.
Do not experiment—it might make trouble. (Essentially a passive position based on the assumption that most things go wrong.)	Feel free to experiment and to take calculated risks—in this way come our greatest successes. (Essentially an active position based on the assumption that most things go well.)

Table 5-4 Two Kinds of Organizational Philosophies *(Continued)*

A Survival-Oriented Philosophy	A Growth-Oriented Philosophy

Problem Solving

Ignore problems and avoid making decisions—the problems may go away without your having to become involved. Justify procrastinating by becoming heavily involved with trivia.	Look for problems and decisions that need to be made—this is what we are paid for.
If you cannot avoid a problem, assign it to a subordinate and assume as little responsibility for it yourself as possible.	See your job as solving problems, but let subordinates help.

Development of People

Do not develop replacements for your job; they may replace you. Your chances of survival are better if the organization contains no ready replacement for you.	Develop replacements—this is the only way you can move up.
Never confront—people do not like it even if it is good for them.	Confront—this is how both parties learn and grow.
Talk a lot about the need *to hire* better people.	Develop and train your own people to be better.
Do not give negative feedback—someone may take offense and harbor resentment that might cause you difficulty at a later date.	People need to know their mistakes if they are going to learn from them and improve their performance.
Get rid of good people by encouraging them to move out of the organization—no point in developing capability if there is no way up.	Train your people so that you become free for bigger, more important things.
Encourage those beneath you to take action. If things go well, you can take the credit; and if things do not go well, they can take the blame.	Be action-oriented yourself. This is the best way to train others to be aggressive.

Table 5-4 Two Kinds of Organizational Philosophies *(Continued)*

A Survival-Oriented Philosophy	A Growth-Oriented Philosophy
Deal mostly on a one-to-one basis. There are no witnesses and no one can point up your inconsistencies and double-dealing.	Deal mostly on a group basis. This is the best way of clarifying inconsistencies and confusion about complex issues.
Personnel evaluations are subjective—does the subordinate keep people happy and not make any problems?	Personnel evaluations are objective—does the subordinate accomplish what is required?
The organization's human resources are consumed and gradually depleted.	The organization's human resources are developed and strengthened.

Environment

Maintain a hard-working atmosphere with no "fat."	Keep enough slack in the system so people can solve problems creatively.
Manage by crisis. My inadequacies are less obvious if there is lots of confusion and frantic activity. Keep people running rapidly.	Manage by plan. The situation will not be frantic and confused if we have planned adequately. Allow people time to plan and stay current with their technology.
Must work only in your own area or peers will work against you.	Resources are readily available to the entire organization.

Assumptions

To get work done, management has to develop methods of controlling people's behavior.	To get good work done, management has to develop methods for releasing subordinates' potential.
Basically people are lazy, unreliable, and uninterested in their work.	Basically people are dedicated, hard-working, and want to do a good job.

The Result of Each Philosophy

Professional suicides and slow organizational disintegration.	Individual and organizational growth.

Table 5-4 Two Kinds of Organizational Philosophies *(Continued)*

A Survival-Oriented Philosophy	A Growth-Oriented Philosophy
Causes	
Often, frightened, insecure people, not sure what they are supposed to be doing, who feel threatened by the accomplishments of others.	Usually, people who feel secure in their jobs and have developed confidence in their abilities as a result of successfully accomplishing increasingly important tasks.

tices that seem more oriented toward short-term survival than development and growth. The behavior of survival-oriented individuals and organizations is highly competitive, highly individualistic, and generally nonsupportive. A growth-oriented organization would have organizational goals and a plan for reaching them and, with the ever-increasing complexity of modern life, would have to emphasize team involvement. (For a further elaboration of this concept, see Table 5-4.)

The organization needed entrepreneurs, people who were energetic and growth-oriented, to keep the organization moving; but managerial control was largely in the hands of custodians—people who were trying to survive, maintain the status quo, and not let the boat rock too much. Although they were needed by the organization, the energetic pushers were rarely protected, let alone valued and rewarded, so that as time passed they increasingly came to be viewed as organizational irritants. Various subtle forms of punishment were invoked until they eventually stopped pushing or left.

The Lack of Interpersonal Competence. Argyris has defined interpersonal competence as:

1. The ability to own one's ideas and feelings

2. The ability to be open to the ideas and feelings of others and to share one's own

3. The ability to experiment and take interpersonal risks

4. The ability to help others to own, the ability to help others to be open, and the ability to help others to experiment.[43]

107

A major problem in the organization is the lack of interpersonal competence by those in managerial control. As an organization grows older and its growth rate begins to slow and perhaps even to decline, those in managerial control may become increasingly threatened by any criticism of their leadership or discussion of organizational negatives. Frank evaluation of the organization and the performance of its members tends to decline. Efforts by individuals to raise problems for resolution are resented, and individuals who do this are subtly punished and accused of having a negative attitude. The ability to confront issues and level with people is reduced in favor of a public relations "sell the management" approach. The intensity of the effort to be positive and the concern about negative attitudes may be directly related to how threatened the organizational leadership is by problem confrontation. Obviously, no organization can be successful for very long if its problems and difficulties have to be denied and the discussion of them cannot be tolerated.

Low interpersonal competence leads to low feelings of one's importance, psychological success, and confirmation by subordinates. To gain feelings of recognition and importance, subordinates may then react by overemphasizing desks, space, technicians, and status as well as by developing norms to minimize openness, conflict, and risktaking. Ultimately, this results in low problem-solving effectiveness on any technical issue that involves the participant's self-esteem or organizational security or both.

As problem-solving effectiveness decreases, the need for people, materials, and time increases. Subordinates' frustration and rigidity in regard to change also increase. At the same time, subordinates' commitment to work and their interest in doing high-quality work decreases, tending to increase costs, which causes dissatisfied top management to react by increasing the pressure to cut costs and by seeking customer feedback. Since the feedback is often negative, it makes top management even more dissatisfied. This, in turn, may lead management to tighten budgets, schedules, and capital expenditures, and to give the customer increased influence.

Workers react by decreasing long-range risky ventures still further. They grow increasingly frustrated and experience further decreases in their feelings of success, essentiality, and confirmation of their technical expertise. This causes increased costs as well as lower morale, lower involvement, higher turnover (of the better researchers), and overemphasis on technicians, space, and flexibility. This again increases management dissatisfaction which, in turn, increases management's emphasis on cost cutting, project evaluation, project control, and "witch hunts," and leads to the creation of a technical ladder. These factors also all feed back to increase costs, which dissatisfies management; and the cycle continues.[44]

As a result, workers are increasingly impelled to become salesmen, overoptimistic in order to get work, and pessimistic about when the job can be completed. They pad their budgets with time and money and learn to write reports that sell a point of view. Managers spend increasing amounts of time on administrative activities designed to pressure and control workers.

The end result is that units begin to fight one another and to protect their sovereignty by developing boundaries. Cooperation and communication decrease and mistrust increases. The practice of hiding bad news from the top increases and so do new projects designed to evaluate researcher effectiveness. This increasing mistrust and lack of communication leads to feedback that supports and reinforces relatively low interpersonal competence. This closes the loop, and we have a self-maintaining system becoming slowly less and less effective and innovative. According to Argyris "the first step toward increasing organizational health is for the top to increase its interpersonal competence."[45]

When the organization repeatedly neglects to act on worthwhile ideas and suggestions for reasons that are never made clear, people eventually stop making them. With the organizational purpose and one's role unclear, the path of least resistance is to wait for clarification. In the absence of performance review, frequently this clarification never comes. And eventually more employees realize they have become professional suicides.

Effects of Certain Existential Beliefs on Management Policy

Kierkegaard (1813–1855) is generally regarded as the originator of Existentialism, which gained prominence in Germany amid the chaos and confusion that followed World War I. It was revived and flourished even more intensely in France during the disorganization that followed World War II. It is a useful philosophy for dealing with situations that are vague, purposeless, and standardless. It was an especially appropriate philosophy for the Resistance movement during World War II because the Resistance fighters had to reject all normal ethical bonds—to family, colleagues, and relatives. Moreover, unlike most martyrs, they could not say what they were fighting for except a vague idea such as "liberty." Rules and traditional standards of conduct were useless, for the Resistance situation was unique and unprecedented.

According to Kierkegaard, no one can know his place, no one can have his duty proved to him, but each must take his courage in both hands and choose as best he can. The creative choice is not the casual decision, after which all goes on much as before, nor the choice "on principle," which subjects the self to an external rule or value and reduces it to identity with other similarly subjected selves. The choice is a critical one that commits one's whole self and one's whole life. The load of responsibility in facing one's own limitations, and especially the ultimate limitation of death, are solely one's own. The fact that people cannot escape death or fall back on other people, rules, or comfortable systems, fills us with dread. Morality thus becomes something wholly beyond reason. There are no absolute values or principles, unless one is to count as the sole value the virtue of "authenticity" or sincerity. Such a theory is particularly appropriate to a time when civilization is breaking up and social bonds have vanished.

The situation in the company under study is somewhat analogous to that in France after World War II. The rapidly changing technology and the rapidly changing business picture made the traditional bureaucratic rules obsolete, and the new ones had not yet been formulated. Because of the newness of the technology, tasks could not be defined, individual charters could not be defined, and the success of jobs could not be defined except in terms of dollars. Management was just not personally competent enough to do this and felt defensive about it.

Confronted by many vague, poorly defined, highly technical problems, management could no longer decide how many employees would be needed, what kinds of training they should have, or even very specifically what they should be doing. To a large extent many of these decisions had to be placed in the hands of knowledgeable subordinates. And this dictated a new kind of management philosophy and the creation of a new kind of relationship (financial as well as psychological) between employer and employee. Certain management policies within the company, which would appear quite outlandish within a traditional bureaucratic frame of reference, can be explained as deriving from certain existential beliefs. Table 5-5 is an attempt to point out management policies resulting from these beliefs.

Present Organizational Strategies for Meeting People's Needs

In the study of professional suicide it is important for us to understand something about the basic needs of people and what provisions the organization makes for meeting these needs. If it makes none, then people will look for nonorganizational ways of meeting their needs (or they may physically leave or psychologically withdraw).

There are essentially three ways in which the industrial organization can deal with the problem of human needs.

1.   It can ignore the problem leaving it to the individual to solve in his own way and, by default, leaving it to the informal organization. (Informal systems within the organizational structure can be remarkably good at meeting the basic human needs, but the result is that employees frequently begin to feel more loyalty and dedication to the informal system and its goals than to the formal system.)

2.   It can place meeting human needs primarily within the context of the larger organizational environment.

3.   It can plan (and train its managers) to meet human needs within the process of the work itself.

By far the most effective method is to have meeting human needs related to the process of work itself.[47] In the organization under study, human needs were largely met within the context of

Table 5-5 Management Policies Resulting from Certain Existential Beliefs

Existentialism developed in France in the disorganized aftermath of World War II and the breakdown of governmental authority and national purpose.	Existential management developed during the technology explosion following World War II and the breakdown in managerial authority as subordinates came to know more about the business than their bosses.

Existential Beliefs	Resulting Management Policy
With the collapse of religion and loss of faith comes a sense of the brevity of life. Thought, institutions, and achievements in general are transitory. The values, goals, and beliefs of society that transcend individual life are meaningless beyond the individual's experience.	If everything is transitory with no real future or purpose, it is pointless to document individual achievement. (No performance reviews and no personnel records kept on achievements.) The only important thing is how I feel at the moment.
The supremacy of reason or rationality is denied. There are strong emotional impulses in human nature which are not to be denied, but recognized and come to terms with.	If the supremacy of reason is denied, then the organization will tend to abandon logically thought out plans in the face of strong irrational emotions.
The direct experiences of life are valued rather than depending on intermediate experiences provided by books, newspapers, reports or computers, etc.	Managers tend to ignore written reports and their conclusions in favor of subjective evaluations arrived at through contact with the persons involved.
Scientific and technical achievements have not solved the problems of man's existence, but instead have increased his difficulties.	There is a tendency to avoid and ignore scientific and technical achievements as not relevant or helpful.
Man is not a ready-made being but becomes *what he makes of himself and nothing more.*	In general, other people in the organization cannot help much. Whatever difficulty people get into (especially professional suicide) is their own doing, and there is little anyone else could do to help.

Table 5-5 Management Policies Resulting from Certain
Existential Beliefs *(Continued)*

Existential Beliefs	Resulting Management Policy
Man's most important choice is between an inauthentic and an authentic existence. Authentic existence means assuming responsibility for one's own existence. Inauthentic existence is the modality of living under the tyranny of the crowd.	Team-building activities may be viewed as subjecting the individual to the tyranny of a group and is thus to be avoided in favor of dealing on a one-to-one basis.
To become authentic, one must deal with existential anxiety, or the recognition that there is essentially no purpose and meaning to life.	Any search for organizational purpose and a meaningful existence is doomed to failure. It is assumed that such efforts are hopeless.
The result for the individual is the acceptance of "nothingness" and spiritual suicide.[46]	The result of existential management for the subordinate may be acceptance of professional suicide. (If existential assumptions are accepted by management, it appears that the problem cannot be solved.)

the larger organizational environment rather than within the process of the work itself[48] (see Table 5-6). When employee satisfactions are provided primarily within the work context and the larger environment rather than within the process of the work itself, there is an obvious tendency for employees to concentrate their efforts in the larger environment rather than finding their satisfactions in the performance of the work.

A Reductionist Theory of Organizations

There are a number of ways of looking at organizations. One way might be called a reductionist theory of organizations. This theory holds that organizations and organizational results are nothing more or less than the result of thousands of individual actions. Implicit in this assumption is that relatively little can be done to change individual behavior (within or outside an organization)

Table 5-6 How Basic Human Needs Are Met

Basic Human Needs According to Maslow	Within the Process of Work Itself (on the job)	Within the Work Environment (at work but off the job)
Physiological needs (food, clothing, shelter)	Salary largely unrelated to quality of work individual performs	Salary set by larger organization and union (not very dependent on quality of work)
Security needs	Security largely unrelated to quality of work	Security arranged for blue-collar workers by union Security for white-collar worker depends on "playing it safe," accumulating seniority, having many social friends, staying out of trouble
Belonging needs	People traditionally placed in competition, staff meetings discouraged as wastes of time, little benefit seen from setting common goals, few incentives for working together	Belonging needs met within larger environment through social clubs and company-sponsored recreational activities
Recognition and self-esteem needs	Occasional merit raises, but because usually not based on evaluation of work, they are viewed as gratuitous. Occasional newspaper articles on contracts being completed, but rarely an evaluation of good work.	Company newspaper articles about social club activities and activities outside organization
Self-actualization needs	Some opportunity to learn new skills on job, depending on individual supervisor No lateral transfers and very little job rotation	Much opportunity to learn new social and recreational skills through company recreational program Opportunity to learn new skills through evening education program Tuition subsidy plan provided by larger organization.

and, as a consequence, organizational results depend on the caliber of the people in the organization. The unsuccessful leader's complaint is that subordinates are not good enough. If they are good enough, they could solve most of the organization's problems on their own.

An alternative view might be called a systems approach to organizational theory. The assumptions here are that organizational behavior is not just the sum of many individual actions, but can be more or less so, depending on how people relate and the structure provided by those in managerial control.

Some organizations (especially those with a policy of internal competition and a lack of goal setting and planning) foster a good deal of canceling-out behavior in which the actions of one member consciously or unconsciously cancel out the action of another. Some organizations, however, provide a team approach for working together, which releases the synergistic effect. This makes it possible for the organization or the team to accomplish more than the sum of what each might have accomplished individually.

The reductionistic assumptions are organizationally self-defeating because management never looks beyond an evaluation of each individual to the systems problems and the leadership problems. A subjective reason for not giving individual performance reviews may be that if this were done, the systems problems and the leadership problems would soon become obvious, and this would represent a threat to the leadership.

A reductionist theory of organizational behavior holds that all organizational behavior can be reduced to an individual, one-plus-one basis, and if anything goes wrong in an organization, it is because some individual (always a subordinate) did the wrong thing.

After studying professional suicides in this organization, it appears that behavior is not just a result of individual personality characteristics, but is highly influenced by role expectations, organizational procedures that place stress on the individual or show care and concern, and the amount of information about the organization that the individual has available.

> The individual employee is always following a sensible strategy for getting along in the kind of world he *thinks* he lives in.
> Rensis Likert

In summary, the lack of more clearly stated organizational goals makes it difficult to plan. The lack of more effective planning makes it difficult to define the jobs that need to be done. The lack of job definition makes it difficult to define charters and who does what. The lack of definition of who does what makes it difficult to review individual performance; and if you do not review performance, it makes it difficult to know who is doing a good job and to give them recognition. Without rewards and some form of recognition, responsible people in time become discouraged. People whose interests and activities are primarily directed toward satisfying their own needs have a great deal of freedom for self-gratification, but those dedicated to improving the organization find fewer and fewer rewards for this dedication and eventually leave the organization or inevitably begin to move toward some form of professional suicide.

The organization placed a great deal of emphasis on providing a self-actualizing environment, apparently forgetting that people are motivated by self-actualization only after their recognition, belonging, security, and survival needs have been met. The lack of team building and the highly competitive atmosphere encouraged by the self-actualization philosophy and the lack of superordinate goals effectively blocked feelings of psychological security and belonging. The lack of organizational goal setting, planning, feedback and performance reviews provided limited opportunities for recognition.

As Presthus points out:

> The upward-mobiles are typically distinguished by high morale; their level of job satisfaction is high. Indeed, the process and criteria by which they are selected insures that they will have an unfailing optimism. The reasons for this are clear. They identify strongly with the organization and derive strength from their involvement. Their dividends also include disproportionate shares of the organization's rewards, in power, income, and ego reinforcement. As we have seen, subjective inequality is a built-in feature of big organization and is rationalized on the basis of equality of opportunity.[49]

But, if (1) organizational values encourage the hiring of a large number of creative, aggressive, upwardly mobile young people, all of whom cannot receive a disproportionately large share of the organization's rewards, and (2) the reward system is not based on contribution to organizational goals (because they have not been defined), and (3) the organization already has a large layer of senior people, which (as eventually becomes obvious) there is no way over or around; then the younger upwardly mobile ones will eventually recognize this, become disillusioned at the difficulty in making any real progress in the organization, and eventually either leave or develop the symptoms of professional suicide.

Not knowing and not being able to find out where one stands generates a great deal of anxiety. Those who handle their anxiety by moving out and doing something eventually do something wrong, which may result in their suicide. Those who absorb their anxiety and passively wait for clarification may also commit suicide, but it usually takes longer and, if the responsibility for action can be placed on a succession of dedicated subordinates, may not have to occur at all.

Notes

1. John W. Gardner, *Self-Renewal, The Individual and the Innovative Society* (New York: Harper & Row, 1963), p. XIV.

2. William Arnold, "The Engineer and His Profession," *Product Engineering,* June 17, 1968, p. 130. A report on the findings of a three-year study at Stanford Research Institute by Howard M. Vollmer, to be called "Handbook of Organizational Design."

3. Donald W. Cole, "The 'Brownie Point' System, A Study of an Organization's Perceived and Idealized Reward System," September 1965.

4. Donald W. Cole, "Evaluation of the Manager Development Program," August 1968. Mimeograph.

5. "Long Range Planning," *Business Management,* March 1967, p. 37.

6. Peter F. Drucker, "There Are No Profit Centers . . . Only Cost Centers," *Harvard Business Review,* Jan.–Feb. 1968, p. 30.

7. Roy D. Waldman, M.D., "Neurosis and the Social Structure," *American Journal of Orthopsychiatry,* vol. 38, no. 1, January 1968, p. 89.

8. Ibid., p. 90.

9. David Mechanic, *Psychological Stress* (St. Paul: University of Minnesota Press, 1930).

10. A. Henry and J. Short, Jr., *Suicide and Homicide* (New York: Free Press, 1954), p. 239.

11. Biderman's "Discussion" of *Cultural Induction to Stress* by Marvin K. Opler in *Psychological Stress,* Mortimer H. Appley and Richard Trumbull (eds.) (New York: Appleton, 1967), pp. 238–239.

12. Bob Conquest, "Community Mental Health," *Announcer,* Cleveland Psychological Association, vol. V, no. 2, January 1969, p. 1.

13. See Chap. 2.

14. Amatai Etzioni, *A Comparative Analysis of Complex Organizations* (Glencoe, Ill.: Free Press, 1961).

15. Warren G. Bennis, *Changing Organizations* (New York: McGraw-Hill, 1966), p. 5.

16. Ibid., p. 6.

17. Ibid., p. 19.

18. Stanley M. Herman, *The People Specialists* (New York: Knopf, 1968), pp. 250–251.

19. E. H. Shils and M. Janowitz, "Cohesion and Disintegration in the Wermacht in World War II," *Public Opinion Quarterly,* 1948, 12, pp. 280–315.

20. Chris Argyris, "How Tomorrow's Executives Will Make Decisions," *Think,* 33, vol. 6, 1967, pp. 18–23.

21. R. Kahn, D. Wolfe, R. Quinn, J. D. Snock, and R. Rosenthal, *Organizational Stress* (New York: Wiley, 1964).

22. Albert Pepitone, "Self, Social Environment and Stress," in Mortimer H. Appley and Richard Trumbull (eds.), *Psychological Stress* (New York: Appleton, 1967), p. 190.

23. L. Festinger, "A Theory of Social Comparison Process," *Human Relations,* 7, 1954, pp. 117–140.

24. R. B. Ammons, "Effects of Knowledge of Performance Survey and Tentative Theoretical Formulation," *Journal of General Psychology,* 1954, pp. 279–299.

25. Robert Presthus, *The Organizational Society* (New York: Knopf, 1962), p. 162.

26. R. B. Cattrell and I. H. Scheir, *Meaning and Measurement of Neuroticism and Anxiety* (New York: Ronald Press, 1961).

27. F. M. Berger, "Control of the Mind" *American Scientist* vol. 55, no. 1, 1967, p. 70.

28. Woodburn Heron, "The Pathology of Boredom," *Frontiers of Psychological Research,* Stanley Coopersmith (ed.) (San Francisco: Freeman, 1964), p. 82.

29. Herbert A. Shepard, "Responses to Situations of Competition and Conflict," *Conflict Management in Organizations* (Ann Arbor: Foundation for Research in Human Behavior, 1961), pp. 33–41.

30. Jerry Harvey, "Some Dynamics of Intergroup Competition," *Training News*, Washington, vol. 8, nos. 3 & 4, Fall–Winter 1964–65, pp. 1–4.

31. Albert Pepitone, "Self, Social Environment and Stress," *Psychological Stress*, page 194.

32. D. Mechanic, *Students Under Stress* (New York: Free Press, 1962).

33. M. Deutsch, "The Effects of Cooperation and Competition on Group Process," *Human Relations* 2: 1949: pp. 129–152.

34. Ed Schein, et al., *Coercive Persuasion* (New York: Norton, 1961), p. 145.

35. J. S. Adams and Patricia R. Jacobsen, "Effects of Wage Inequality on Work Quality," *Journal of Abnormal and Social Psychology*, 69: 1964, pp. 19–25.

36. Schein, *Coercive Persuasion, p. 156.*

37. Ibid., p. 209.

38. Thomas C. Schelling, *The Strategy of Conflict* (New York: Oxford University Press), pp. 170–171.

39. Israel Goldiamond, "Moral Behavior: A Functional Analysis", *Psychology Today*, vol. 2, no. 4., September 1968, p. 34.

40. Carl Pacifico, "Advice for Mismanagers," *Chemical & Engineering News*, Mar. 18, 1968, vol. 46, no. 13, p. 116.

41. "Analysis of the Omicron Company," Ann Arbor: University of Michigan, 1964. Mimeograph.

42. Goldiamond, "Moral Behavior," p. 33.

43. Chris Argyris, *Organization and Innovation* (Homewood, Illinois: Irwin, 1965).

44. Ibid., p. 240.

45. Ibid.

46. Cofer & Appley, *Motivation Theory and Research* (New York: Wiley, 1964), pp. 657–658.

47. Frank Friedlander, "Job Characteristics as Satisfiers and Dissatisfiers," *Journal of Applied Psychology*, 48, 1964.

48. F. Herzberg, B. Mausner, and B. Snyderman, *The Motivation to Work* (New York: Wiley, 1959).

49. Robert Presthus, *The Organizational Society* (New York: Knopf, 1962), pp. 167–168.

six

Relevant Research

To achieve insight into the origins of a disease
is by no means the same as to discover an
effective therapy, but it is certainly one of the
necessary conditions for this.[1]

There are a number of studies in psychology and sociology that
may help in more adequately understanding professional suicide,
the ineffective utilization of creative talent, and some of the
causes. They include the classic study on suicide by Emile Durkheim, the sensory deprivation studies by Hebb, studies of concentration camps and POW camps by Biderman and Mayor, the
studies by Sherif on group conflict and cooperation, and various
studies on animals by Liddell (conditioning emotions), Masserman (experimentally induced neuroses), and Brady (ulcers in
executive monkeys).

From research that has already been done, we can draw certain
tentative conclusions about professional suicide—what is destructive to people and also what they need to remain healthy and
work productively.

Durkheim has impressive statistics to support his belief that
suicide is a sociocultural phenomenon rather than an individual
psychological pathological phenomenon. He found suicide closely related to the individual's degree of integration into the social-
psychological environment. If integration is too loose, egoistic or
anomic suicide follows, either because the ego is not constrained
and channelled or because a sense of purpose in life is lacking. An
individual who is too tightly integrated and "committed," may

become involved in committing altruistic suicide of a sacrificial nature.

We can speculate that the professional suicide of the bright young employees we studied could have been materially reduced if more attention had been paid to integrating them into their respective groups through a more precise definition of group goals. Instead of working on group tasks, many were sent off with individualistic charters to which the organization was not committed and in the final analysis would not support.

From the isolation studies we can see that people need stimulation and sensory input. When isolated and alone, they eventually develop pathological reactions. While the in-depth analysis of their symptoms may prove interesting, the most helpful treatment is for someone to put them back in touch with reality.

From the prisoner-of-war and concentration camp studies we can see that in groups under great stress for survival, it is usually the predator and the ruthless who gain control of the resources in short supply and are, consequently, the ones to survive. Unless groups have developed a strongly cohesive spirit before being placed under severe stress or unless they can find a leader to unite them, only a few will survive, because the predatory ones will consume a disproportionate share of the limited resources. In addition, many people would rather die than continue to live in a situation that violates certain cultural and social values important to them.

From Sherif's experiments on group conflict and cooperation, it can be seen that trust and cooperative behavior follow the establishment of superordinate goals rather than vice versa.

Liddell's experiments with sheep show that destructive reactions to stress are greatly increased if the subject has no rationale by which to understand what is happening. It is not so much the pain of the stress as it is the inability to comprehend the complexity of the pattern that is most destructive. It also appears that stress can be reduced if there is someone nearby in whom the subject has confidence. Thus, we can see that when subjected to a lack of input (sensory deprivation), confused input, or inputs that make them feel alone and insecure, subjects suffer gross distortions of reality, with resulting performance deterioration.

From Brady's experiments with ulcers in "executive" monkeys, it seems that stress is greater when the inability to decide correctly adversely affects others.

Durkheim's Study of Suicide

The classic study of suicide was done by the French sociologist, Emile Durkheim, in his book, *Le Suicide.* Durkheim collected extensive statistical data from all over Europe which then became the basis for systematically rejecting traditional theories that attributed suicide to such things as mental alienation, race, heredity, national climate, temperature, and imitation. Showing the individual and nonsocial causes to be irrelevant, he then defined three kinds of suicide—egoistic, altruistic, and anomic—and their causes.

Egoistic suicide results from the lack of integration of the individual into society. Durkheim found that the suicide rate of a society increases as the forces throwing individuals onto their own resources grow greater. For example, in times of great crisis the suicide rate falls, according to Durkheim, because society is then more strongly integrated and individuals are more actively involved in social life. When their egoism (individualistic freedom) is restricted, their will to live is strengthened.

In an organization with a philosophy of management by individual commitment, the egoism of the individual has great room in which to move. According to Durkheim, the suicide rate would be expected to increase under a type of management philosophy in which individuals are provided with great freedom to do what they think best. We found trends in this direction, reflecting the high proportion of people who cannot live without attachments to some object or idea for which they have strong feelings and which will outlive them. Some find life intolerable unless the group with which they are allied wants them to exist and gives them some purpose to justify coping with life's many problems. Individual interests alone are not a sufficient end for activity. Many people must find something bigger than themselves for which to live. An organization that regards its employees as being in the organization only for their own self-interest (except when needed for day-to-day crises) may find many of its bright, young people who want to feel dedicated to something greater than themselves moving dispiritedly toward organizational and professional suicide.

Durkheim also found that children, old people, and (to a lesser extent) women—whom he sees as more self-sufficient than men— rarely commit suicide. He postulated that because men are complex social beings, they can maintain their equilibrium only by finding points of support outside themselves. It is because their moral balance depends to a greater extent on others that they are more easily disturbed and more likely to commit suicide than women. One reason people commit suicide is that they lack sufficient reason for living. Those who are "other-dedicated" and need to gain a sense of self-completion through something outside themselves are more likely to commit suicide than those who are self-sufficient.

Altruistic suicide results from individuals taking their own lives because of some higher commitments, which may involve either religious sacrifice or political allegiance. In our study we found people who, because of their commitment to a task, were doing things that they must have known would only result in their own destruction. Durkheim says that both egoistic suicide and altruistic suicide may be considered symptomatic of the way in which individuals are structured into society. In egoistic suicide situations, they are inadequately structured into society. In altruistic suicide situations, they are so overinvolved that they accept and continue in a situation personally destructive to them.

Durkheim's third type of suicide is called "anomic suicide." "Anomie" is a chronic problem in modern life and results from the lack of regulation of the individual by society. Traditionally, the individual's needs and satisfactions have been regulated by what Durkheim calls the collective conscience. When this regulation of individuals is upset so that their horizons are broadened beyond what they can endure, or contracted unduly, conditions for anomic suicide increase. For example, sudden wealth, Durkheim says, stimulates suicide on the grounds that newly rich individuals are unable to cope with the new opportunities offered them. Similarly, in divorce a spouse no longer exercises a regulative influence upon the partner and suicide for the divorced person is comparably high. This situation is more severe among divorced men than among divorced women because, according to Durkheim, it is the man who is most regulated by the influence of marriage.

In a society of rising expectations, people's desires can frequently outstrip their ability to satisfy them. When expectations are limited, happiness is somewhat secure because it is defined, and a few mishaps are not disconcerting; however, by striving for too much, one can find oneself in a state of perpetual frustration. "To pursue a goal which is by definition unattainable is to condemn oneself to a state of perpetual unhappiness."[2]

Many of the young employees in this study were in pursuit of goals that were held out as possibilities but which, on more sober reflection, appear to have been quite unrealistic. The frustration of striving for something that seems to be coming no closer was destructive to them (and to the organization, because it eventually deprived the organization of their abilities). They illustrate Durkheim's findings that the drive toward suicide is not so much a function of the individual as it is a function of society. It is the social structure of the group, not the individual characteristics of people, which is important in determining the rate of suicide. Although individual behavior patterns can be described once the three kinds of suicide have been established, Durkheim found that suicide statistics available to him were not correlated with biological or individual personality phenomena, but with social phenomena. It is the collective conscience, the totality of beliefs and practices, folk ways and customs, that are essentially responsible for high or low suicide rates. For Durkheim, the suicide rate was symptomatic of a basic flaw in the social fabric of the culture.

In concluding, Durkheim suggested certain antidotes. Egoistic suicide can be reduced by reintegrating the individual into group life through the reestablishment of occupational groups and compact voluntary associations, and the establishment of common superordinate goals (that is, team building). Superordinate goals, goals with which the *entire* organization can identify, serve as an integrating force around which individuals can rally. Altruistic suicide can be reduced by being more realistic about the kinds of demands made on people. Anomic suicide can be reduced by being realistic with individuals about how much is reasonable for them to expect to accomplish (through periodic performance reviews and career counseling). Chapter 7 will discuss how the conditions that create suicide can be alleviated through such things as management by a philosophy of group commitment, participation in T-group training, team building, goal setting, and career planning.

Experiments on People in Isolation

The effects of environmental conditions on individuals have been graphically demonstrated by D. O. Hebb, a psychologist at McGill University.[3] Begun in 1941 under a grant from the Defense Research Board of Canada, the study involved subjects who were paid $20 a day to lie on a comfortable bed in a lighted cubicle 24 hours a day for as long as they cared to stay. Visual, auditory and tactile sensations were severely limited by protective devices. In the preliminary run, most subjects had planned to think about their work, review studies, plan papers, and so on; but nearly all reported that the most striking thing about the experience was that they were unable to think clearly about anything for any length of time and that their thought processes seemed to be affected in other ways.[4] On almost every test, the subjects' performances were impaired by their isolation, and also the content of their thoughts gradually changed. First, they tended to think about their studies, then they began to reminisce about past events. As time went on, the subjects became increasingly irritable. Eventually, after long isolation many of them began to hallucinate. Hallucinations were not only visual, but auditory and tactile as well.

The results of these studies indicate that some input of sensory stimuli from the environment is essential for mental efficiency in human beings. Without this input the brain ceases to function adequately, and behavioral deficits and abnormalities begin to develop. Not only is thinking impaired, but the individual also becomes irritable, shows childish emotional responses, develops disturbed perceptions, loses the sense of perspective, and suffers hallucinations. Many developed a mild sense of paranoia. They felt that those in control of their environment were against them and were trying to make things tough on them. We might say that under conditions of severe isolation the individual's perception of reality can become so impaired as to constitute a temporary psychosis-like state.

The effects of social isolation and professional isolation on people have been less systematically studied. We do know that isolation is usually perceived as a form of punishment and is remarkably effective. In our prisons, isolation is the punishment saved for the most recalcitrant of criminals, and very few can stand it for long.

In a study of apartment house occupants it was found that when people live geographically close to one another without meaningful communication, gross distortions of perception occur.[5] Schutz and Argyris report similar findings from industry when meaningful communication is absent.[6,7]

Many of the young people in this study were isolated—not physically, but occupationally and psychologically. The many social events sponsored by the company could not occur often enough to compensate in any substantial way for the loneliness and social isolation of being committed to goals that others did not appreciate or even understand. Over a period of time, those headed for suicide frequently developed gross distortions in their perceptions of reality.

Groups Under Extreme Stress for Extended Periods

For humanitarian as well as practical reasons, it is difficult to subject large groups of people to extreme stress for extended periods. Consequently, there are few scientific studies of this subject. However, studies have been made on the basis of reports in retrospect of prisoner-of-war camps and concentration camps in which groups of people have lived under extreme stress for extended periods. From these studies something can be learned about what happens to individuals, as well as to groups, when they are subject to prolonged stress.

Repeated observations made by former prisoners and observers describe how, under the pressure of extreme deprivation, "men became like animals." Social scientists have come to use

more sophisticated terms such as "deculturalization," "desociali-
zation," and "depersonalization" to describe people who have
been reduced to the animal level, but the essential meaning remains much the same. Under conditions of deprivation, the fight
to have a need met can become so all-consuming that ethics and
codes of morality lose their force. In prison camps it was the fight
for bread that meant survival. In modern industrial organizations
the problem is not physical but psychological survival, and the
coinage is not food but recognition. In organizations under great
stress, recognition is a scarce commodity and there is much competition for it. In industrial organizations it is the fight for acceptance and respect and accomplishment that may determine one's
professional survival.

One conclusion Biderman draws from his studies of captive
groups is that group survival is a goal towards which prisoners
may organize themselves when they perceive the situation as
marginal, that is, when all seem to have a good chance of surviving provided there is concerted action toward the goal of group
survival.[8] Organization of prison communities does not evolve or
quickly breaks down, however, where conditions are submarginal
or perceived as submarginal by a significant number of the group,
that is, when it seems apparent that there is just not enough to go
around and not all will survive. When the dominant question
becomes "Who shall survive?", organizations resting on voluntary cooperation cannot contend with general disorganization or
"clique organization."

Biderman goes on to say that official inmate organizations
concerned with the welfare of the entire group lose control because of their inability to control major rewards and sanctions.
And their loss of control is accelerated by the capture of key
positions and materials by cliques. In groups under extreme
stress, a number of cliques generally arise that contend with each
other and with the official inmate organization. As the organized
but unofficial cliques gain control over the food, weapons, and
bartered goods, they increase their physical strength and their
power positions, while at the same time the less dominant groups
grow weaker.

"A predisposition towards psychopathological ruthlessness
does not appear inevitably necessary for the membership of

cliques which succeed in such circumstances, but it is not necessarily a hindrance."9 Although there have been some major exceptions, groups of criminals have come out on top with frightening regularity. Noncriminal groups that have succeeded in submarginal situations have generally been those that operated according to an equally ruthless doctrine, but have justified it in terms of some more selfless social value. Elites, in order to survive or to pursue some larger purpose, must be willing to appropriate a disproportionate share of food and other materials. Obviously, it is only in exceptional circumstances that this can be done by any kind of general consent. Those who serve the purpose of the controlling organization or merely help maintain its power, must be provided with more than a subsistence ration. This requirement involves a more or less deliberate decision to force others to accept starvation, cold, going without medicine, performing debilitating work; or, in the case of German concentration camps, the filling of quotas for the gas chamber. Leadership in submarginal situations, therefore, requires as its base a commitment to some objective other than the survival of the group as a whole. Principles must then be developed toward which leaders are willing to sacrifice others as well as themselves. Organization of prison populations towards such objectives as escape and resistance arise more typically in situations of relative abundance than in submarginal situations.[10]

Exploitation of prison populations by predatory subgroups is characteristic of submarginal situations. These predatory groups can markedly accelerate the rate of death for the mass of prisoners, since very small losses of rations, clothing, and shelter can prove fatal. They can also create an atmosphere that greatly increases the proportion of the group choosing by conscious or unconscious acts not to engage in the fight for survival at all—those who succumb because of the apathetic, fatal withdrawal frequently noted in submarginal captivity.

Biderman points out that the breakdown of social, intellectual, and cultural controls hinders the use of intelligence, foresight, and insight by individuals for their own survival. It also contributes to high fatalities by reducing the cooperative functioning of prisoner groups that is necessary for the survival of any considerable portion of their members.

A second characteristic in large groups subject to chronic and extreme deprivation is that some proportion of these groups is reported to have perished because they lost the will to live, rather than as a direct result of starvation or chronic disease. The most common interpretation of such "fatal surrender" (other than moralistic interpretations regarding the weakness of character of those who succumb in this way) is that the behavior necessary for survival demands violation of cultural norms, to which the individual is unwilling to agree even when his survival depends on it. Many people failed to survive because they failed to become decultured and desocialized—because they chose not to live at all, rather than to live like animals.

Not only were some prisoners unwilling to snatch, cheat, and steal to get food, but in some situations, they also refused to set aside certain cultural inhibitions and sank into starvation rather than eat perfectly edible strange foods that were available. For some people in such settings the primitive urge to survive is not powerful enough to overcome certain acquired moral and ethical standards.

Biderman goes on to point out that death is also a psychological event, as the inmates of mental hospitals can testify. The social and cultural destruction of a person can occur without his biological death. It is clear from the studies of many prisons that in some situations a drastic disintegration of social involvement and culturally relevant behavior may be necessary for physical survival. In many situations a correlation appears to have existed between the survival chances, health, and recuperation of a captive on one hand and, on the other hand, the ease and rapidity with which he could disinvolve himself socially and shed much of his cultural equipment. Studies of groups under stress show that in order to survive one must find some way of meeting the physiological, social, and cultural necessities.

An alternative to either becoming predatory or committing suicide is a third possibility best illustrated by the Turkish soldiers in the Red Chinese prisoner-of-war camps. According to Mayor, they were all captured in the early stages of the war, and all were either sick or wounded. In sharp contrast to the Americans of whom for every 10 captured 4 died, 100 percent of the Turks survived. How did they accomplish this? First, when one got sick, the others cared for him, fed him, bathed him, washed his clothes and kept him warm. Second, they had strong group loyalty and rigid group discipline toward their goal of group survival. This was in sharp contrast to the Americans, whose survival was expressed in such private terms as "my survival is going to be my affair, buddy, and yours is your private affair. You leave me alone and I'll leave you alone." Third, the Turks had a chain of succession. Recognizing the need for leadership, when one leader was removed, another rose to take his place and he was obeyed without question.[11]

Some say the Turks survived because there was less pressure on them from the Red Chinese. Certainly the Red Chinese did not have as much to gain by converting Turks as they did by converting Americans. But others conclude that the Turks survived because they had a strong cohesive unit due to prior training. They had strong leadership with a commonly accepted means for filling the vacancies that occurred, and they had superordinate goals accepted by all members of the group.

While it may seem unreasonable to compare the stress of a Red Chinese prisoner-of-war camp with the stress of modern industry, the example may teach us something about how situations of extreme stress over long periods may be dealt with most successfully. And there may be implications for the prevention of professional suicide in the example provided by the Turkish soldiers.

Experiments in Group Conflict and Cooperation

Sherif has used groups of boys at a summer camp to experiment in intergroup conflict and cooperation. He first had the group engage in competitive activities such as tug-of-war, baseball, and football. As a result of this competitive play, each group became increasingly hostile toward the other. Later the groups were put to work on a common task with meaning for all of them, which could not be accomplished easily by either group alone—such as finding a leak in the line of their common water supply or starting a stalled bus to go for food for both groups. He found that when two groups have conflicting aims, so that one can achieve its ends only at the expense of the other, members of one group will become hostile to members of the other group even though each is composed of normal, well-adjusted individuals. While the effect of intergroup conflict was to increase solidarity, cooperativeness, and morale within each group, this did not carry over to the group's relations with the competing group.

From these studies Sherif concludes that intergroup conflict and its by-products of hostility and negative stereotypes are not primarily a result of neurotic tendencies on the part of individuals but occur under certain conditions even when the individuals involved are normal, healthy, and socially well adjusted. Contact between hostile groups, even when they meet as equals, does not in itself necessarily reduce conflict between them.[12]

However, contact between groups that involves interdependent action toward common superordinate goals *is* conducive to cooperation between groups. Single episodes of cooperation are not sufficient to reduce intergroup hostility and negative stereotypes once established, but a series of situations involving cooperation toward the groups' superordinate goals has a cumulative effect in reducing intergroup hostility.

Managing by subordinate commitment tends to heighten hostility and interpersonal and intergroup conflict because of the competitiveness it fosters and the relative lack of superordinate goals that have been established and are being worked on together.

Stress Studies of Animals

To obtain insights into the behavior of human beings, especially that connected with their innate drives and conflicts, it is often helpful to study the behavior of less complex animals. There are a number of studies done with animals which may help us understand the process by which employees become professional suicides. Experiments with animals obviously cannot provide wholly satisfactory answers, but animals can be studied under controlled conditions, and it is through animal experiments that some scientists find leads to the effect of emotional stress on more complex organisms.

An important contribution to the understanding of neurotic, self-destructive, irrational behavior is the work done by Liddell at Cornell on sheep and goats. In an effort to test the intelligence of sheep whose thyroid glands had been removed, they were timed as they went through a maze. It was assumed the sheep traveled the maze to receive the reward at the end, but it was noticed that some sheep appeared quite uninterested in the reward and seemed to run the maze for the sheer joy of accomplishment.

On one occasion a pistol was fired over the head of a normal sheep just as it reached a turn in the maze. It was able to complete its task of getting through the maze, but on subsequent trips through the maze it would be very anxious, balk, and run in the wrong direction when it got to the spot where the pistol had been fired.[13]

In our study individuals were found who apparently had been traumatized in the past and would suddenly, at a certain point in their careers, balk and begin to take steps in an inappropriate direction. Although they were usually able to continue functioning and to complete their tasks, they did so with greatly decreased effectiveness.

In another experiment Liddell found that sheep could be conditioned to raise a leg in response to a mild electric shock, with no ill aftereffects as long as the pattern of the shocks remained relatively simple. However, when sheep were subjected to the same mild shocks in a more complex pattern, one they could not easily anticipate, they became "neurotic." They exhibited every evidence of alarm by bleating, labored breathing, and repeated movements of the head and ears. Even when tested while resting in the barn at night their heartbeat was found to be rapid and irregular. The neurotic sheep would be easily startled even by slight noises and were severely agitated upon entering the laboratory. Some refused to nurse their young. More seriously, they seemed incapable of dealing with danger in any realistic fashion. One sheep that had been made experimentally neurotic by this method, instead of running off when dogs approached, as did the others, was found crouching on the ground with a foreleg extended, which the dogs had chewed to the bone. Once established, the experimental neurosis affected not only the animal's behavior in the laboratory but also its way of living in the barn and the pasture. This was not just a temporary condition but lasted for 24 hours a day the rest of its life.

Pavlov is reported by G.V. Anrep to have conducted a similar experiment in which an experimental neurosis was produced in a dog as a result of its inability to distinguish a circle (as a signal for food) from an oval (signaling no food). When the oval approached a circle so that the dog no longer could distinguish between them, it exhibited a dramatic emotional upset. It barked and squirmed in its harness and could not be quieted. Apparently behavior can be profoundly influenced (in a negative direction) and subjects can become extremely upset when they are subjected to even mild discomforts that they are unable to comprehend. A management that does not clarify its goals and its policy of working toward those goals (and especially if it does not clarify its punishment system) will find people becoming upset whenever it becomes obvious to them they do not understand.

Liddell reports that they have studied more than 50 sheep and goats with experimental neuroses and have never found a permanent cure for this condition. They tried "rest cures," keeping the animals out of the laboratory for as long as three years; "change of scenery," moving to another laboratory on a much larger farm; "change of job," through careful retraining with a lighter schedule; even injections of an extract of cortin into the andrenal cortex—all to no avail. Liddell concludes that prevention is the best therapy. Their principal research objective now is to determine in detail what features of the animals' training program are most stressful and what can be done to increase resistance to these stresses. Some of the people in our study reacted as though they had been subjected to an "experimental neurosis" conditioning process, and when we study the history of their experiences, we can see that all of them have received some form of negative conditioning.

In another experiment by Liddell, twin sheep were subjected to identical stress with the exception that one sheep had its mother with it during the stress and the other did not. The sheep that had its mother near during the shock seemed to be unaffected by this experience, while the sheep that experienced the shock alone developed neurotic symptoms.

One of the most detrimental effects of management by subordinate commitment is that individuals are often left alone and isolated to experience their shocks by themselves. "As long as I leave you alone, you should know that you are doing all right" (a common remark made by bosses). It is customary for people moving toward professional suicide to be largely ignored by their bosses until there is a crisis. People moving toward professional suicide become isolated from their peers because they are so busy or are seen as threats, or both.

Paradoxically, Liddell reports that a signal indicating no shock is to be given was found to be more disturbing to the sheep than the positive signal. An uninterrupted series of negative conditioned stimuli was repeatedly found to result in experimental neurosis for the sheep. Liddell concludes that actual pain, when confidently anticipated, leads to the relief of painful emotional tension.

For humanitarian reasons these experiments could probably not be conducted on human beings, so there will always be some question about how applicable they really are. There is the suggestion, however, that shocks can be tolerated if the rationale for their application is known. But, more important, if the rationale for being even mildly shocked is not known, it can prove very upsetting and can be destructive to performance, not only in the short run, but also in the long run. It is for these reasons that open communication is so important to the health of organizations.

If Liddell's experiments with sheep can be applied to people, the antidote would appear obvious. Provide employees with a theoretical framework that will make comprehensible to them the rationale for the shocks they receive as an inevitable part of being in an organization, and provide bosses with good communication skills so that significant information is readily communicated.

Experimentally Induced Neurosis

Experiments with animals help illustrate in anecdotal form some problems common to people. Jules Masserman, in working with cats, describes how they could learn to obtain food pellets by prying up the lid of a food box. The animals were then taught to wait for various sound and light signals and to manipulate various switches. If the training was too rapid for the cat because of its age or intelligence, the cat would become recalcitrant, inept, and resistant. If the training was properly adjusted to the individual cat, however, its behavior would be efficient, well integrated, and successful; and it would have all the characteristics of a happy cat as demonstrated by its eagerness to enter the laboratory and to purr while it worked for its reward.

After having been thoroughly trained to get food by flashing a light and then ringing a bell, these animals could be made neurotic by occasionally subjecting them to a mild shock or a blast of air just as they were to receive rewards. Masserman reports that animals treated in this fashion exhibited rapid heart rate, catchy breathing, raised blood pressure, sweating, and trembling. They showed extreme startle reactions to minor stimuli, became irrationally fearful of physically harmless sights and sounds as well as closed spaces, air currents, vibrations, caged mice, and even food itself. They developed gastrointestinal disorders, recurrent asthma, sexual impotence and muscular rigidities resembling those in human hysteria and catatonia. Peculiar compulsions emerged, such as restless, elliptical pacing and repetitive gestures and mannerisms. Masserman reports that one dog, after such conditioning, could never approach his food until he had circled it three times to the left and bowed his head before it. These neurotic animals lost their group dominance and regressed into excessive dependence and helplessness.[14] In fact, they displayed many of the same stereotypes of anxiety, phobias, and regression under stress as those observed in human beings. (I am reminded of several managers in this study who, after years of hard work,. were suddenly shocked to find an organization that they had worked so long and so hard to develop suddenly sold off or given to someone else to manage without a reasonable explanation. Their reactions to this sudden shock of not getting something which they felt they had been promised were not very dissimilar to those of the experimental animals.)

In another experiment two cats, each of whom had been taught to manipulate a lever to obtain food, were placed in a single cage—but the cage was so constructed that the cat that manipulated the lever could not get to the food box until after its companion had eaten the pellets. Under these circumstances some cats formed a cooperative effort in which they would alternately work the lever and collect the food. However, this usually did not last very long. Sooner or later one of the cats would refuse to work the switch but be on hand to eat the food. The "worker" cat finding its efforts unrewarded would eventually stop working the switch. Both cats would then loll around the cage for hours. However, as hunger mounted, the undernourished cat working the switch would usually discover that if it worked the switch very rapidly it might produce enough food so that a little would be left for it before the "parasitic" cat ate it all. It was found in these experiments that the worker animal had to work very hard for a meager living while the parasitic cat lived in luxury. Interestingly, these cats rarely become hostile to one another. The only conditions under which the animals fought was when one was displaced from a position of social dominance to which it had become accustomed or after it became neurotic.

It would appear that the sudden, angry, self-destructive acts of some of the managers in this study may have been the result of such so-called neurotic behavior. Following a long period of psychological starvation, which resulted from a parasite boss who consumed all the psychological rewards from the subordinates' work without sharing, the subordinate would suddenly retaliate in some personally destructive way.

Cats that had been taught to obtain food by subjecting themselves to mild electric shocks would exhibit extreme forms of suffering and masochism. If they had been trained thoroughly enough to do this, the cats would inflict greater and greater electric shocks on themselves in an effort to get the reward they had been taught could be obtained in this manner. Similarly, managers who had been taught that hard work would gain organizational rewards would subject themselves to more and more punishment in the hope that rewards might be forthcoming, sometimes completely exhausting themselves in the process.

Ulcers in Executive Monkeys

Various investigators have been able to produce ulcers in experimental animals by subjecting them to physical stress, but Brady was the first to produce ulcers in animals through psychological stress. Monkeys were placed in a cage where they were subjected to a shock every 20 seconds. They could avoid this mild shock if they pressed a lever at least every 20 seconds. It does not take long for a monkey to learn that it can avoid shocks by manipulating the lever. Next, two monkeys were teamed up. Both monkeys received the shock, but only one monkey (which we will call the "executive" monkey) had a lever that could prevent shocks. Both monkeys were, thus, under the same physical stress, but only one was under the psychological stress of having to press the lever properly in order to protect them both from shocks. After 23 days of continuous 6 hours on and 6 hours off, the executive monkey died. An autopsy revealed a large perforation in the wall of the duodenum. An autopsy on the other monkey showed it to be in good health with no gastrointestinal abnormalities. Other experiments using the same methods produced the same results. The executive monkeys developed ulcers and the others did not.[15]

If we can make an analogy from executive monkeys to industrial managers, it would seem that there may be a special stress on those whose inability to decide correctly causes hurt to others. Many of the managers in this study had such decision-making power and were deeply concerned about the hurts that their inability to decide correctly caused to others. A management philosophy of subordinate commitment, by placing responsibility for the individual's problems on the individual, may have been an attempt to protect conscientious bosses from the executive pain that resulted from their contribution to subordinates' pain. An alternative, however, would be to develop more team effort by which everyone on the team shares responsibility together for the inability to always decide correctly.

The next chapter will discuss some specific ways in which the problems of stress and the incidence of professional suicide might be reduced.

The old, the learned, the powerful, the wealthy, those in authority—these are the ones who are committed. They have learned a pattern and have succeeded in it. But when the change comes, it is often the uncommitted who can best realize it, take advantage of change in general and of industrialization in particular. The uncommitted younger sons, barred from success in the older system, are always ready to exploit new opportunities. In Japan these younger sons were treated more indulgently by the parents and were given more freedom to choose an occupation since, in Japanese folk wisdom, it is the younger sons who are the innovators.[16]

Notes

1. Konrad Lorenz, *On Aggression* (New York: Harcourt Brace & World, 1963), p. xi.

2. Emile Durkheim, *Suicide* (New York: Free Press, 1951), p. 248.

3. Woodburn Heron, "The Pathology of Boredom," in Stanley Coopersmith (ed.), *Frontiers of Psychological Research* (San Francisco: Freeman, 1963).

4. Ibid., p. 83.

5. Source unknown.

6. William C. Schutz, "Interpersonal Underworld," *Harvard Business Review,* July–August 1958, pp. 123–135.

7. Chris Argyris, "T-Groups for Organizational Effectiveness," *Harvard Business Review,* March–April, 1964, pp. 60–74.

8. A. D. Biderman, "Life and Death in Extreme Captivity Situations," Bureau of Social Science Research, Washington, April 1967.

9. S. Wolf and H. A. Ripley, "Reactions Among Allied Prisoners of War Subjected to Three Years of Imprisonment and Torture by the Japanese," *American Journal of Psychiatry,* 104, 1944, pp. 180–193.

10. The failure of well-organized, predatory inmate groups in Korea to prosper by extortion from fellow prisoners differentiates the Korean case from the situations which developed in various Civil War prisons, the German concentration camps, Russian prisoner-of-war camps and slave labor camps.

11. William E. Mayor, M.D., "Brainwashing," an address before the Freedom Foundation, Taft Broadcasting Company, Cincinnati.

12. Muzafer Sherif, "Experiments on Group Conflict and Cooperation," in Harold J. Leavitt and Louis R. Pondy (eds.), *Readings in Managerial Psychology* (Chicago: The University of Chicago Press, 1954), pp. 408–421.

13. Howard S. Liddell, "Conditioning Emotions," *Scientific American,* January 1954.

14. Jules H. Masserman, "Experimental Neurosis," *Scientific American,* March 1950.

15.   Joseph V. Brady, "Ulcers in Executive Monkeys," in Stanley Coopersmith (ed.), *Frontiers of Psychological Research,* pp. 250–255.

16.   Warren G. Bennis, *Changing Organizations* (New York: McGraw-Hill, 1966), p. 27.

seven

The Antidote

Even in the unlikely event that every supervisor
could acquire a sincere and understanding
attitude toward each of his men, boredom and
inefficiency would remain . . . The frontiers of
human productivity already lie beyond decent
supervisory relationships. This is why the more
recent research on motivating environments has
focused on the organization itself, on the
distribution of power.[1]

Motivation does not lead to achievement; rather
it is achievement that leads to motivation. The
inappropriate attitudes that we find in
employees are a product of the way we use
people.[2]

You owe no loyalty to your employer other
than not betraying secrets. Be ruthless about
finding out whether you belong.[3]

In order to avoid professional suicide, in order to be effective,
and in order to lead useful, satisfying lives, people need:

1. A purpose and a goal
2. Resources for accomplishing the purpose:
    a. people resources (hands and brains)
    b. material resources (paper and a place to work)
    c. intellectual resources (technology and training to do the
    job)
    d. emotional resources (someone who cares)

3.   Communication and feedback on how they are doing

4.   Support and encouragement (and a sense of personal worth)

5.   Enough freedom from work overload and anxiety to learn new things

A survey of 3,000 engineers in 140 companies throughout the United States by William E. LeBold shows how content engineers are with their jobs is governed by:

1.   The manner in which their skills and abilities are used

2.   The degree to which opinions may be expressed freely

3.   The extent of backing and cooperation received from superiors and others

4.   The kind of treatment accorded to them as professionals

5.   The opportunities provided for keeping up with developments[4]

Pressures on the organization and on the individual tend to allow little time or attention for these important needs. Failure to have these needs met causes stress for the individual and eventually results in a lack of organizational accomplishment. Although the organization needs sacrificing, dedicated employees who will fight a status quo system to accomplish what must be done, it frequently does not do enough to protect the very persons it most needs.

> The purpose of life is to matter, to be productive, to have it make some difference that you lived at all.[5]

Specific Recommendations

Following are a number of steps that might be taken to reduce the incidence of professional suicide and to increase the effective utilization of good people:

1.   Establish specific organizational goals. This will reduce the nebulous character of organizational objectives and provide a framework against which the relative priorities of personal goals can be established.

Someone has said that managing is the art of integrating organizational goals with personal goals. Obviously, if organizational goals are only vaguely defined or kept hidden and personal goals are not discussed, their integration will be difficult. The stress of nebulous situations can best be relieved and the sense of purposelessness and anomie counteracted by organizational and individual goal setting. Surplus energy, which is sometimes used destructively in playing games, can only be harnessed if goals are provided.

Much has been made of the need for more trust and collaborative behavior (instead of distrust and competition) if an organization is to succeed. However, as noted earlier, the works of Sherif show that collaborative behavior *follows* the establishment of superordinate goals rather than preceding it.[6] Not only will goal setting reduce the ambiguity in the system, allowing more energy to be directed toward organizational objectives, but the establishment of superordinate goals will also reduce the competitiveness between people and release energy for collaborating toward common organizational objectives.

The mediocre and the insecure are going to resist exposure to the withering challenges of a no-nonsense work environment where goals are set and results are measured. Such people much prefer "the jungle" where their mediocrity can be hidden by under-the-table maneuverings. Organizational goals will provide some support for the dedicated ones in their struggles with the status quo custodians and the predators.

2.   Develop a plan for meeting these goals. This will require some definition of the role to be played by various individuals and the clarification of their charters. ". . . to meet a problem, you should start by understanding the problem; you should look at alternate approaches; you should attempt to estimate the value of the various approaches; you should break it down into its pieces and insure that the pieces are put together to constitute a harmonious, optimum ensemble."[7]

3.   Initiate team-building activities and develop a leadership style of managing by group commitment. As a result, individuals' needs can be met within the process of the work itself rather than in the larger context of the work environment. This is more

effective. Team-building around superordinate goals will reduce competition and will encourage building collaborative supporting relationships.

The environment for today's managers has become so specialized and so large that the ad hoc coming together of chance contributors is no longer an effective way to function. Under a leadership style of managing by subordinate commitment, the most aggressive tend to dominate regardless of their competence, and there is a tendency for the less aggressive to let them do this. Even worse, those managers who are weak at decision-making find it easy to wait until the majority has made up its mind and then jump on the band wagon. Management badly needs to make better use of behavioral science technology for building teams and developing more collaborative environments if more effective and more profitable solutions are to be found.

4. Initiate achievement (performance) reviews at regular intervals to evaluate the good work being done, and initiate a reward system based on organizational results rather than rewarding psychological one-upmanship or the ability to dominate a meeting.

5. Initiate training programs in interpersonal competence to teach the skills of owning, leveling, and experimentation. This will improve communication, provide opportunities for more effective solutions to problems, and provide feedback on the quality of the results so further improvements can be achieved.

Past success no longer ensures future success. It is important to foster the development of a growth-oriented rather than a strictly survival oriented environment. Because of the impact of the top boss's philosophy on the organization, and because no one is perfect, contact with and some reeducation of this boss will be required. It is also important to train for management in depth so that when growth opportunities occur a cadre is available to capitalize on them.

6. Someone in the organization, most logically the person at the top, needs to assume responsibility for clarifying the rules of the game, the reward system and what it takes to get ahead.

Organizations that have grown rapidly tend to evolve in disorganized ways. Procedures developed from past practices become increasingly incomprehensible to the newcomer, as tradition and past favors play an ever-increasingly important part in decision making. If there is little hope for fair play, after a time it becomes an every-department-for-itself, everyone-for-himself affair. Someone in the organization must have assigned responsibility for seeing that those who are willing to work hard and make sacrifices for the organization are protected and not destroyed by organizational members who feel threatened. Bosses have expected that individuals, out of personal commitment, would take responsibility for improving the organization and that the satisfaction of meaningful work would be sufficient reward all by itself. Dedicated individuals will take initiative on their own for improving the organization, but this is too important a function to go unrewarded and to leave to individual chance.

Improving a very complex industrial system for more effective task performance is a highly specialized job requiring highly specialized skills and a special charter to deal with organizational resistance. Organizations have become so complicated, and there is so much inertia and organizational pressure exerted toward maintaining the status quo, that attempts to modify the organization through informal contacts among peer groups is no longer a workable solution. System improvement and organizational development cannot be done by an isolated unit of one or two individuals buried deep in the organizational bowels with only filtered communication to the top. Legitimate ways must be developed to communicate directly to those in managerial control, for without formal recognition and without help from the top, relatively little can be accomplished.

7.   Opportunities must be provided for decompression and the periodic release of stress and frustration. This can be accomplished through conference attendance, vacations, and T-groups.[8]

The most effective technique so far found to prevent professional suicide has been that associated with the sensitivity training of T (training)-groups. When caught up in the syndrome of professional suicide, what the individual needs most is a friend.

Yet it is at this time that most business acquaintances instinctively draw back because they do not want to be tainted by association with a failure or because they are uneasy about how to handle the situation.

It is essential that the enlightened organization provide opportunities for conference attendance and education. Because of the knowledge explosion, individual knowledge banks must be continually updated. And not only must these opportunities be made available generally, but periodic checks must be made by the organization to see which employees are not taking advantage of these educational opportunities. It is easy for committed individuals to get so involved with their jobs that they do not keep updating their knowledge. Because of its importance, not only to the individual but also to the organization, some form of organizational scrutiny should be maintained over this. For people in high-pressure jobs, a plan that provides only two weeks of vacation per year for the first 10 years (and these are frequently the high-pressure years) is completely inadequate.

8. Reduce the anxiety in the system. While anxiety is a great motivator, the results tend to be at rather primitive levels of creativity and innovation.

Anxiety can be reduced by goal setting and by being as clear as possible about purpose and function. It is recognized that goals cannot be perfectly defined, but formal organizational efforts should be made to establish definitions.

9. A skills inventory should be established for each employee, and the organization should maintain a work force planning effort.

Confidential studies by several large companies I know have demonstrated beyond serious question that a substantial proportion, often as many as one-third, of those tagged promotable by their supervisors lack the talents required for those higher-level jobs! This, of course, raises an ominous question about those deemed *not* promotable by their supervisors. There is typically little check on those passed over for promotion—except turnover![9]

10. Ongoing studies are needed as a means of continually promoting organization improvement and correcting organization deficiencies.

A program for routinely monitoring the organization and regularly compiling exit interview data should be established. Exit interview data is not only helpful in itself, but because of the highly stressful nature of the environment many people who leave the system have had an extreme experience in failure and have experienced a real challenge to their self-concepts, and may need some professional help in coming to grips with their feelings.

Effects of Professional Suicide on the Organization

There is always a certain amount of grieving and mourning when anyone leaves an organization, but in the cases of professional suicide, it is greatly intensified. The individual who commits suicide sentences the survivors to thinking over and over about his suicidal death. Suicides leave their skeletons in the survivors' psychological closets. No other kind of death creates such lasting emotional scars as does suicide. A rationale is needed for the survivors in order to free them from these scars. The cost of each suicide in terms of its effects on the survivors is extremely difficult to ascertain, but there certainly is a cost to organizational morale as well as to the mental health of the survivors.

A company's task of maintaining a mentally healthy environment becomes clearer if we recognize that at each stage in employees' life careers they are exposed to hazards, conflicts, perplexities, and sometimes overwhelming demands and frustrations, for which they can and should be strengthened, and from which, as far as possible, they should be protected. Frank points out that in promoting mental health we are concerned with how individual personalities can be strengthened to meet life's tasks, not by solving but by reformulating their problems (which as personalities, they create for themselves) and by reorienting their customary ways of seeking the goal values of our traditions and their often self-defeating ways of striving for their aspirations.[10]

Healthy personalities are to be viewed as individuals who continue to grow, develop, and mature, accepting the requirements and the opportunities of each successive stage of life and finding the fulfillments this offers without paying too high a cost personally or socially, as they participate in maintaining social order and carrying on the business of the organization.

Management by group commitment requires a different kind of leadership style from that being practiced in most organizations. Although industry's aversion to decision by committee is well known, more efficient forms of group participation have become increasingly necessary. Certainly the traditional authoritative boss-follower relationship is no longer suitable, since most of the know-how necessary to run an organization effectively and profitably can no longer be expected to rest within one person. A formal boss role results in reticent, submissive, defensive, and even withdrawal behavior on the part of the group.

Anderson has pointed out that a parliamentary or democratic system is also not suitable, since it is based on the assumption of debate and opposition.[11] The leader is required to abdicate his role as a participant so that he can act as referee and procedural adjudicator. Members of the group tend to form lobbies, pressure strategies are devised, and coalitions are formed to achieve personal goals, often at the expense of total group performance.

For a group to be successful in the highly complex environment of today, new strategies of leadership style and group problem solving must be devised. If we can train managers in a cooperative approach to problem-solving, in which the combined intelligence of all members could be brought to bear on the problems, the duplication of effort and the energy wasted in competitive game playing can be avoided.

Team success requires that:

1.   Members must have some idea of what is the problem to be solved. (It is amazing how many potential problem solvers in a group have no real understanding of the problem.)

2.   Members must have a general appreciation for one another and their potential contribution to the problem to be solved.

3.   Members must have some ability to understand one another's

language and be able to translate this knowledge into activity where relevant.

The principal task of problem-solving discussion leaders is to keep the team directed toward the logical order of problem identification, problem solutions, and action decisions. In this role, their task is neither to govern nor to mediate disputes, but to listen to and observe the group process and keep the team directed toward the problem. The leader relates comment to comment, seeks clarification, summarizes various suggestions, and redefines the problem until consensus is reached. A group member should be available as reporter to keep track of the decisions made both in the short term (at the meeting) and longer term (what was it we decided?). The longer term record should be written and available for all members to read and correct.

The members' obligation in group-committed problem-solving teams is to concentrate on the group problem and the group process rather than on individual defensiveness or status seeking (which is so common, perhaps even inevitable, in management by subordinate commitment). One method for training subordinates in this new kind of role is T-Group training in which individuals develop some appreciation for and understanding of group processes and of their impact on others. Another is to rotate each group member through a consultant role where individuals have to extract themselves from the content of the discussion in order to listen and to deal with the process going on in the group.

To reinforce the move toward greater self-control, a system of goal-oriented achievement reviews would be introduced for each individual. In such a program, individuals would be encouraged to set goals relating to their personal development as well as to their contributions to the team. Periodic reviews would be directed toward giving support and encouragement to people so they can learn from their actions, rather than setting up controls and communication constraints in the system, which inhibit growth, reduce knowledge of results, and increase fear and anxiety.

A review in which a supervisor or manager works with a subordinate to establish realistic joint goals that are later reviewed to determine progress is a form of positive control. A supervisor who, without prior mutual agreement on goals, tells subordinates that their actions are wrong provides an example of negative control.

As people become more professional and highly valued, it will be increasingly necessary to fit the job to the person rather than the person to the job. To better fit the needs of individuals into the overall needs of the organization, it is important that they be given opportunities to express their changing wishes for new and different assignments. One way of doing this is to have open posting of jobs. In this way, individuals can express directly their need for new assignments as they become available. They can also find out what education or skills are necessary to qualify for certain work and can begin to prepare themselves in a realistic way for more significant contributions to the organization. A system such as that just described would require a different mode of communicating and interacting from what has been traditional in most organizations.

Social-Cultural Needs Met by Perpetuating Professional Suicides

Before the antidotes for professional suicide are put into effect, it is important to define the needs that are met by perpetuating professional suicides. Unless the needs being served by professional suicide can be met in some less destructive way, it is unlikely the antidote will be used.

There are advantages for the organization in perpetuating professional suicides. People involved in professional suicide become legitimate outlets for the inevitable frustration and aggression occasionally felt with regard to one's job. It is generally considered illegitimate to criticize one's boss or management; so the presence of a person involved in professional suicide provides a socially acceptable scapegoat outlet for feelings of frustration and hostility. People in an organization that does not give performance reviews need a basis for comparison to evaluate themselves. A few professional suicides scattered through the organization reassures people in very capable groups that they are good and making a contribution, because they are so much more effective than X. If X were helped to be more effective, it would by comparison reduce their public image; so there is often resistance from peers to rehabilitating a person previously labeled ineffective. Often, the only alternative is for X to leave.

People are frequently surprised how effective X can be in a different setting, provided the deteriorating effects of the previous suicide have not become too ingrained. There is a very real limit to the number of people who can fight a fire at any one time or who can work toward organizational goals without some role definition. Moment and Zaleznik discovered that when a group of stars are brought together, one emerges as "star" and one emerges as "underchosen"—even though in another group the underchosen may have played the star role.[12]

The presence of a few professional suicides provides negative role models. Managers personalize the roles for those who learn best from positive examples. Professional suicides become the examples from which others are taught how not to behave, thus providing a legitimate social-cultural educational function. (This does meet a social-cultural need of which the victims are sometimes aware and it does focus attention, of a sort, on them even though very destructive in the long run.)

Prevention

There are three levels for preventing professional suicide:

1. Primary prevention: establishing an environment in which it would be unnecessary for suicides to ever occur.

2. Secondary prevention: effectively treating individuals caught up in the suicide process.

3. Tertiary prevention: reducing the amount of disability in the survivors, the mourning time, the residual guilt, and the proneness to future mental illness.[13]

Primary prevention requires the establishment of a managerial climate and a psychological environment that support organizational accomplishment. In the organization under study, the environment supported individually competitive relationships. The lack of trust and the fear of risk taking in an environment that seemed to emphasize second-guessing, and a crises-reactive orientation to problems, resulted in people becoming survival-oriented. The relative lack of support and goals all contributed to the suicide of good people.

Secondary prevention requires that aid stations of qualified people be established to interrupt the suicide process. Personnel people and those in line positions must be trained to recognize the problem and the symptoms of professional suicide, to understand its characteristics and dynamics, to help alleviate the stresses, and to make appropriate referrals (which requires a knowledge of referral resources).

Practically all suicidal behaviors stem from a sense of isolation and from feelings of some intolerable emotion on the part of the victim. By and large, suicide is an act to stop an intolerable existence. In order to halt suicides we have to understand what "intolerable" means to another person. Obviously this is different from person to person. Very few suicides occur without some hint of what is to take place. If we want to save these people, we must become better at hearing their hints.

Tertiary prevention requires that managers receive the training and acquire the skills to confront issues before subordinates become suicides. High energy people, new to the organization, are likely to ignore company traditions unless they are very careful. Animosities and misunderstandings can arise that perpetuate unless confronted and dealt with. Some managers leave confrontation to peers and hope that the new employee will catch on in time. But, in a highly competitive environment peers are sometimes not very helpful and avoid the orientation role.

An integral part of the climb out of suicidal depression is one's faith and the faith of surrounding individuals that one is going to make it. Just as hopelessness breeds hopelessness, hope breeds hope. In a highly competitive culture hope is sometimes hard to find.

There are many possible approaches and most of them have already been touched upon. Sometimes a structural change is indicated, and many gradations of approaches lie in between. The best organizational lubricant will probably always be an ability on the part of each individual to accept the others as they are. Many tensions and difficulties become manageable in a setting of mutual acceptance and emotional security, which would rip a more hostile and defensive group wide open.[14]

Plainly, management must be willing to examine itself and, where necessary, to experiment with new methods of organization. But that is not all, management must also acquire a better understanding of the individual worker, what motivates him, how he got that way, and why he behaves as he does.[15]

Unless we cope with the ways in which modern society oppresses the individual, we shall lose the creative spark that renews both societies and men. Unless we foster versatile, innovative and self-renewing men and women, all the ingenious social arrangements in the world will not help us. Finally, we shall renew neither ourselves nor our society, nor a troubled world unless we share a vision of something worth saving.[16]

Notes

1. Saul W. Gellerman, *Motivation and Productivity* (New York: American Management Association, 1963), p. 94.

2. Frederick Herzberg, reference unknown.

3. Peter Drucker, "The Psychology of Managing Management," *Psychology Today,* March 1968.

4. William E. LeBold, "Keeping Engineers Content," *Engineer,* July–August 1967, p. 16.

5. Leo Rosten, reference unknown.

6. Muzafer Sherif, "Experiments on Group Conflict and Cooperation," in Harold J. Leavitt and Louis R. Pondy (eds.), *Readings in Managerial Psychology,* (Chicago: University of Chicago Press, 1964).

7. Simon Ramo, *Forbes,* May 1, 1967, p. 57.

8. Chris Argyris, "T-Group for Organizational Effectiveness," *Harvard Business Review,* March–April 1964.

9. Arch Patton, "The Coming Scramble for Executive Talent," *Harvard Business Review,* May–June 1967, pp. 155–171.

10. Lawrence K. Frank, "The Promotion of Mental Health," *Mental Health in the United States,* The Annals of the American Academy of Political and Social Science, vol. 286, March 1963, p. 169.

11. W. D. E. Anderson, R. W. Quirk, et al., "Industrial Change—Challenge and Opportunity," *The Journal of Industrial Engineering,* vol. XVIII, no. 10, October 1967, p. 579.

12. David Moment and Abraham Zaleznik, *Role Development and Interpersonal Competence* (Cambridge, Mass.: Harvard University Press, 1963).

13. Edwin S. Shneidman, "Preventing Suicides," *Bulletin of Suicidology,* National Institute of Mental Health, Washington, December 1968, pp. 19–25.

14. "Further Reflections on Conflict Management," in Elsie Boulding (ed.), *Conflict-Management in Organizations* (Ann Arbor: Foundation for Research on Human Behavior, 1961), p. 56.

15. Gellerman, *Motivation and Productivity,* p. 97.

16. John W. Gardner, *Self-Renewal, the Individual and the Innovative Society* (New York: Harper & Row, 1963), p. xiv.

eight

Summary

. . . proper management of the work-lives of human beings, of the way in which they earn their living, can improve them and improve the world and in this sense be a Utopian or revolutionary technique.[1]

This study is concerned with the problem of professional suicide and the process whereby bright, talented young people, after a relatively brief time with an organization, become ineffective by either suddenly leaving the organization or not performing according to expectations. It was thought by management that this problem was a result of some kind of pathological process going on within the individual. The findings of this study indicate that the problem is not so much within individuals as between individuals and the organizational environment in which they are expected to work and be productive. It had been anticipated that management might not be altogether pleased with the results of a study that traced the problem of professional suicide to the work environment and the organization's philosophy of management.

The relationship between emotional problems and environmental problems has long been known. Harry Stack Sullivan once observed that schizophrenia is not so much a disease as a way of life. For over a century, all efforts to understand and treat mental illness as simply the breakdown of a diseased mind have failed. The famous Swiss psychiatrist, Paul Eugene Bleuler in his classic work, *Dementia Praecox,* focused attention on the fact that "external circumstances play a major part in shaping the development of an individual's psychological derangement." And Adolf Meyer, who popularized the term "mental hygiene," was impressed with the importance of environmental factors in the development of schizophrenic states and developed a comprehensive view of mental illness based on the relationship between individual and environment.

It was recognized, theoretically, that many problems might be related to the emotional climate within the organization and that any efforts to correct problems of professional suicide would have to consider the climate aspect. However, it was less clearly recognized that the top boss in an organization is the one largely responsible for setting its psychological climate, and any in-depth study of the problems created by this person's style of management could be threatening.

Because the organizational goals were not clear, because the plan for reaching those goals had not been established, because priorities had not been determined, and because charters were not clear, a tug of war ensued between the individual desires and wishes of many different persons and the limited resources of the organization. In this tug of war, the most persuasive and the most ruthless tended to win. An organization that is fatalistic will accept the outcome of countless tugs of war as the best result possible, but I must question if there is not a better way of achieving organizational results. Obviously, these many tugs of war resulted in the expenditure of much energy that might have been better used than against one's teammates. Also, they resulted in the loss (or suicide) of those who did not relish this kind of life or who were not very adept at it.

Unclear, overlapping charters result in competition between individuals over who does what. The expectation held by management that these individuals can resolve their own problems without management's help creates further difficulties, because individuals who cooperate with peers on crucial decisions may later find they have lost out to someone who refused to cooperate.

Without someone in charge, those who cooperate for the good of the organization may be taken advantage of, while those who refuse to cooperate get more of what they need. There is little recognition for good work well done, because good work is never specifically defined. In addition, longer and longer working hours lead to mental fatigue and less-creative problem solving. After a time, symptoms begin to appear. Noncommitted individuals find some means other than the organization's work to meet their psychological needs, and the committed people begin to feel more and more unappreciated and deprived.

Some of the problems noted in people in the very early stages of professional suicide are:

Unrealistic goal setting

Development of severe anxiety

Input overload

Problems around lack of interpersonal skill

Linkage failure

Alienation

The assignment of unclear charters and the urgings of bosses that subordinates take more and more responsibility without commensurate authority and resources generally results in subordinates overextending themselves and establishing unrealistic expectations for themselves. Setting unrealistic goals and expectations makes people anxious, makes them work longer hours, and deprives them of the satisfactions of achieving realistic goals.

Again, because of unclear charters and the lack of organizational boundaries for individual responsibilities, subordinates invite or accept an unrealistic amount of stimulus input. As a result, feelings of fatigue develop, with a periodic need to "decompress." Individuals rarely recognize how tired and overextended they have become until they leave the organization for a more relaxed environment, where they discover that they are able to do little else but sit and think.[2]

Because of the pressure under which people are operating, they tend not to take the time to perform the small courtesies that are so much a part of maintaining a cooperative environment. Linkage failures result from insufficient time being spent on their maintenance.

Gradually, the individual becomes more and more alienated from the environment, detached and uninvolved. With alienation comes performance deterioration and greater isolation from the organization.

The symptoms of professional suicide are those listed in the first chapter:

1.   Some suddenly quit for other jobs far beneath their abilities —a sudden effort to escape a destructive environment. Because they have been beaten down by the system, they feel unqualified for jobs equal to their capabilities.

2.   Some suddenly become disruptive—an effort to break out of isolation and regain lost self-esteem through some impulsive act. Or perhaps, having become isolated, they are no longer fully aware of what is disruptive or organizationally unacceptable. And some, unable to make the decision to leave for themselves, force the organization to make it for them by committing some serious blunder.

3.   Some quit working and retire on the job—a refusal to fight for an organization that seems not to care. Others, caught with unclear charters in a highly competitive environment gradually deteriorate under peer group competition and psychological one-upmanship.

4.   Some get caught in a flurry of crises and become slowly obsolete. They express their anxiety by becoming so committed to day-to-day-crisis tasks that no time is taken for their own self-renewal and educational updating.

5.   Some develop psychosomatic complaints—under the stress and anxiety of coping with a poorly defined environment there is an erosion of physical health.

6.   A few were found to be so caught up in their own and the organization's anxiety that they had great difficulty in slowing down and, in spite of stern urgings from their physicians, seemed headed toward physical suicide.

Along with other symptoms goes the problem of wounded self-esteem. The boss's expectations are that the charter can be accomplished with little authority delegated and few resources assigned. Out of respect, subordinates tend to accept the boss's evaluation. With lack of success comes wounded self-esteem.

There are many ways in which individuals try to deal with this loss of self-esteem; one way is through suicide.

The process of professional suicide and the various phases through which it progresses have been studied and are now fairly predictable. They include:

1. The acceptance of a vague charter

2. A honeymoon period

3. Informal testing of individuals and their charters by peers and subordinates to see if they have management's backing.

4. Conflict within individuals over their charters and the boundaries of the charters.

5. The search for support or resolution from the boss (the formal system).

6. Search for support from peers (the informal system)

7. Symptom formation

The permissive management approach fostered under management by subordinate commitment leaves people feeling neither free nor committed. In fact, permissive management is probably the most controlling technique a supervisor can use—all under the pretense of noncontrol.[3] The permissive manager implicitly invokes the controls of the supervised and creates the scary world of nonlimits. Few people can exist in a limitless world.

Lack of reciprocity (which is characteristic of permissive management) causes many individuals to be cautious in setting limits for themselves; they tend not to chance unilateral failure. Continued lack of meaningful feedback ("You're doing fine, keep up the good work") often prompts individuals to reset their limits closer and closer.

In sum, permissive management can have an effect quite opposite to the one it professes to have. Rather than affording individuals maximum freedom, the supervisory vacuum invokes their controls and encourages them to set "safe" limits—which become increasingly safer and more constricting.

In any organization there are at least three systems that must be mutually supportive and congruent for the organization to function smoothly and effectively. These systems are: (1) the highly personal system of values, attitudes, and beliefs that people carry around in their minds; (2) the informal system that informal groups support; and (3) the formal system of those things people do because the organization requires it. A major problem in all organizations is the way these systems work at cross purposes and cancel one another out rather than being mutually supportive. For example, companies may put plaques on the wall about what their bosses say they believe, but both the formal and the informal systems may not support and may even subtly punish people who act on these statements.

For an organization to be effective, it is necessary to develop a system of attitudes, beliefs and expectations that support organizational members in doing their best, without expecting so much that members wind up becoming suicides. This is achieved through orientation, training and "leveling."

The informal system, through group rewards for organizational achievements, should support individuals in doing what the organization needs to have done; while the formal organizational system must establish policies and procedures that not only support but also reward the achieving of organizational goals. The formal organization must also provide the means for the integration of many varied individual efforts toward common organizational objectives.

Various efforts have been made to increase organizational effectiveness by working within each system, but to achieve any real results, efforts must be made to improve all three systems. A major problem in management by subordinate commitment is that the efforts of dedicated workers committed to improving the organization are not supported by policies and procedures within the formal system that adequately integrate the efforts of many such people toward clearly stated organizational objectives.

A major impediment to organizational improvement is the tendency for management, and personnel people in particular, to view organizational problems as individual personality problems. There is a strong reductionistic tradition in Western thought that systems can be subdivided into functional parts, that each can be studied more or less isolated from the rest, and that criteria for improvement of each can be established with little, if any, reference to the remainder of the system. C. West Churchman, among others, has emphasized the special need today to view and understand whole systems and parts of the systems.[4] Someone in the organization must have a conception of the organization as a whole.

Instead of placing emphasis on building a system that would support organizational objectives, the organization under study relied heavily on charismatic leaders who (on an individual commitment basis) worked toward goals that they themselves thought important. These people were expected to use minimal authority (organizational leverage), and organizational resources were kept tightly controlled by the bosses.

There are a number of disadvantages in relying primarily on charismatic leaders for organizational accomplishment; for example, Headlee found that compared with realistic leaders, they cannot tolerate strength in their surrogates, enlisting instead almost total "homoerotic commitments."[5] Also, with group goals undefined and with heavy reliance on the individual goals of numerous subleaders, an intraorganization competition is established. As a result, tremendous amounts of energy, which might better be channeled toward organization goal accomplishment, are consumed in politicking and behind-the-scenes maneuvering. Synergism becomes impossible.

Another disadvantage is that with the increasing complexity of the world, no one person can beat the system for very long. When an individual with minimal or no authority, minimal support, and few resources accepts responsibility for moving a large organization relying primarily on personal magnetism, the end result is frustration, stress, and the professional suicide of good people.

One of the problems in an achieving society is that no one is ever satisfied. People struggle harder and harder, and the more they get, the higher they set their goals. There appears to be a constant relentless pressure of having to do more and more and never being satisfied. This is particularly true of managerial ranks. The absence of structure is an important negative. The extent to which things can be routinized is the extent to which people's minds can be freed for more creative pursuits.

It is important to realize that to the employees in this study, a job was more than just a way of earning a living. It was daily proof of their worth and importance. To the committed individual, life without accomplishment is not worth very much. The dedicated would rather lose all, because without all one has very little. Self-esteem in U.S. industry is based on "delivered usefulness," not as in Europe where it is based on birth. As a result, useful work becomes extremely important to people. Those who grow accustomed to trivial work and cease to complain about the boredom of their jobs are the least capable. They accept because they have no place else to go. We tend to kill off the best because their competence directed along new channels irritates us (examples are Socrates and the psychodynamics of Christ's crucifixion).

> Everywhere men are praying for a larger challenge of their powers, a larger testing, which may give a larger assurance of their value in the whole great adventure of existence. They are seeking not the line of least resistance, but the line which offers the maximum certainty of personal worth per unit of effort extended.

Problems in the Study

There were a number of factors that handicapped this study. Chief among them were:

1.   The lack of performance reviews in the organization and the difficulty of ascertaining with any degree of objectivity who was in fact ineffectively utilized

2.   The lack of a precise definition of professional suicide and an organization-wide statistical count that would indicate whether the rate was going up or down

3.   The lack of a control group to determine whether the apparent reduction of suicides was due to some of the procedures indicated or to a net loss in the total number of bright aggressive people who were most prone to professional suicide

4.   The lack of organizational support for the project, requiring its continuous justification through the assumption of numerous ancillary activities

5.   The lack of adequate secretarial assistance, making precise record-keeping difficult

We do not pretend that our conclusions are based on an exhaustive analysis of all young executives in the company who committed professional or organizational suicide. Rather, we built a theoretical analysis around a relatively small number of individual cases. The reason for this was the difficulty in disguising persons' identities.

A characteristic of some organizations is that they seem to require professional suicides for movement to take place. Too little is done to protect the creative people who have the most to contribute. The jobs of the entrenched are protected, and it appears that one becomes entrenched by supporting and maintaining the status quo.

In essence, the process of professional suicide is one in which people with high achievement motivations are brought into the organization, given vague charters, and asked to commit themselves to tasks not always fully understood by organizational personnel. Assurances are given that the organization values the individuals, that opportunities for achievement and growth are present, and that their contributions will be noticed.

Following employment, managers develop a "hard-bargaining" stance in an attempt to squeeze out as much work and allocate as few resources as possible. Competition between individuals is subtly encouraged as a means of developing a hard-working environment. Only over a period of time does it gradually become clear to these hard-working people that most of the good assignments go to the same people, and the reasons for this are difficult to understand. Rewards appear to be given not on the basis of objective criteria or results accomplished, but rather on the basis of subjective evaluations and personal relationships.

It appears from this study that professional suicide is not really suicide at all; rather it is the result of the slow torture and eventual failure that dedicated individuals go through in attempting to do something for an organization that has not been able to define what it wants and that perpetuates an informal system quick to retaliate against those seen as threatening and not conforming to traditional patterns.

Top management evolved a means for managing the organization, which to them appeared benign yet reasonably effective. Unfortunately, what was intended (and the view down through the organization) was not the same as what people actually experienced (and the view up through the organization). This book is about what people actually experience.

Although a number of steps have been defined that might be taken to reduce the incidence of professional suicide, it is unlikely that any real progress will be made until:

1. Top management becomes more interpersonally competent; better able to own, level, and experiment, and more able to help others to own, level, and experiment: "The first step toward increasing organizational health is for the top to increase its interpersonal competence."[6]

2. Top management becomes more willing to set specific goals and to plan for the accomplishment of these goals and to share more of its authority and its rewards.

3. Top management becomes more growth-oriented and less survival-oriented (see Table 5-4).

4. Top management develops a management philosophy based on team commitment and on a growth orientation rather than legitimizing a self-actualizing predatory environment for those individuals who are oriented primarily to their own survival and their own personal interests.

5. Peers become less fearful of bright young talent and more aware of the contribution they can make to the achievement of organizational goals, with a resulting greater sense of achievement for everyone.

An organization with a philosophy of management by subordinate commitment and a system of interaction based on individual competitiveness cannot compete successfully with an organization with a philosophy of management by group commitment and a system of interaction based on cooperativeness, because there is less opportunity for a synergistic effect. Under management by subordinate commitment, one plus one frequently equals zero or, at most, two. Under management by group commitment, one plus one equals three or more.

The difference between the success and the failure of a corporation lies in the way management treats its human resources. . . . It is important that industry show the same resourcefulness and ingenuity in social dynamics as have been shown in marketing and in production.[7]

Notes

1. Abraham Maslow, *Eupsychian Management* (Homewood, Ill.: Irwin, 1955), p. 277.

2. The feeling is similar to that reported by an ex-Marine combat sniper in the Painesville, Ohio *Telegraph* of November 1, 1967. "On those days off everyone developed a feeling of nothingness. You could sit for hours doing nothing and if you tried to write a letter, you couldn't think of a thing to say."

3. Frank Jasinski, "Permissive Management," Thought Paper, July 29, 1968.

4. C. West Churchman, *Challenge to Reason* (New York: McGraw-Hill, 1968).

5. Raymond Headlee, M.D., "The Nature and Nurture of Charisma," *Transactions,* Department of Psychiatry, Marquette School of Medicine, Milwaukee, vol. 1, no. 1, Spring 1969, pp. 13–17.

6. Chris Argyris, *Organization and Innovation* (Homewood, Ill.: Irwin, 1965), p. 240.

7. W. P. Gullander, "The Age of Industrial Sophistication," in Alan McLean (ed.), *To Work Is Human: Mental Health and the Business Community* (New York: MacMillan, 1967), chap. 2, pp. 12–24.

The Study of Professional Suicide

The management in one division of a large aerospace corporation became concerned about the number of bright young engineers and scientists who, after several years of promising service with the organization, would suddenly, over a few weeks or months, take steps that led their careers with the organization in a negative direction. This process, referred to as professional suicide, happened in several ways:

1. Some quit their jobs for other jobs far beneath their ability.

2. Some became disruptive and did things for which (management assumes) they must have known they would be fired.

3. Some quit working and gradually retired on the job.

4. Others, caught up in the flurry of daily crises, did not keep up with the rapidly changing technology and after a period of time, found themselves outmoded and obsolete.

During the course of the study, three more types were discovered:

5. Those who developed physical complaints of a classically psychosomatic type such as headaches, ulcers, and backaches. (Alcoholism, readily identified by the community as a form of professional suicide, was infrequently found among this group of middle class managers, engineers, and scientists; possibly because individuals who solve their problems with alcohol probably never

got promoted to this level, or at least had enough experience in masking their problem so that they were rarely discovered.)

6.   Some, after having been highly productive in the past, were placed in jobs where, for various reasons, they were grossly underutilized. Unable to resolve these problems with their boss and unwilling to quit, they quietly began to deteriorate under the constant feelings of being regarded as inadequate by their peers.

7.   Those who seemed headed for physical suicide.

Management first discussed this problem with a psychoanalytically oriented psychiatrist. His immediate reaction was, "What you need is a psychiatric social worker, someone trained in clinical observation of the relationship between the emotional problems of your people and the environment you organize for them."

The choice of an applied social scientist was a unique decision. In the division of skills on the traditional orthopsychiatric mental health team, it was the psychiatrist who was the medical and neurological expert, the psychologist who was the testing expert, and—while time has tended to blur these differences somewhat—the psychiatric social worker who was the sociocultural environmental expert. On this basis, he was the most logical of the mental health professionals to work with these industrial mental health problems. In Europe there are a great many social workers employed by industry. In America, industrial social work is so poorly developed as to be almost nonexistent, and thus not recognized as a resource for solving management problems.

While management did have a humanitarian concern for its employees, it was felt that changes in the individuals' attitudes and behavior would lead to increased effectiveness on the job. Thus, it was sophisticated self-interest rather than improved mental health per se, that provided the budget justification for the establishment of this industrial, orthopsychiatric mental health project. Because organizations are composed of people, there was also the implicit assumption that many problems in an organization result from the unsolved problems of a few people dispersed throughout the organization.

Because of the dependence on government contracts, widely

fluctuating employment levels, and higher management's lack of awareness and support of the project, work on this project was recognized as a risky career choice. However, management developed a powerful argument. They said, "Knowing the length of time it takes to be of significant help to the underprivileged and the traditional social agency–clinic population, you can, if you want, spend the rest of your life working with them. Or, we offer you the opportunity of working with bright, young, highly educated people—people who would rarely go to a clinic or social agency for help, but who, with relatively smaller amounts of help, can have a significant impact on our society."

I wish I could say we were smart enough to anticipate all the problems that the project would encounter. In an organization where the professional suicide of bright, dedicated people had become obvious enough to need a project to study it, difficulties could be expected. We were aware that if there were adverse fluctuations in the business or if the project were to become sufficiently misunderstood by higher management, it might be suddenly terminated. We were prepared for this. In the design of the project, a psychiatrist was to be made available on a regular continuing basis. He was to function on a consulting basis from outside the organization, where he would be less subject to the strains and stresses of the organization and where he would be available to provide some greater measure of objectivity to the project. It was also hoped that he might provide to those associated with the project some measure of protection against their own professional suicide.

This seven year project was divided into five overlapping phases (see Figure A-1). Although each phase had a major emphasis lasting about a year, most of the activities mentioned overlapped one another. In retrospect, it appears that phases I and II were essentially diagnostic phases during which the problems of bright young men committing professional suicide were analyzed. Phases III, IV, and V were essentially treatment phases during which efforts were made to correct the basic problems of a psychologically unhealthy environment.

Although this study was originally established to reduce the incidence of professional suicide within the organization and referred to as "A Study of Professional Suicide," the title later

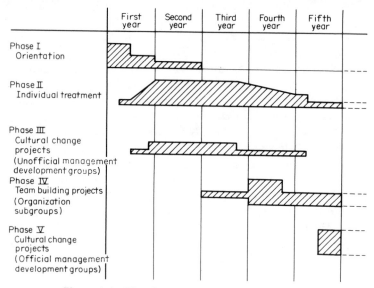

Figure A-1 The phasing of various project activities.

changed to one thought to be more positive sounding, "The Effective Utilization of Creative Talent."

Phase I

Phase I was a survey-orientation phase. Shortly before the program began, the organization had just completed an extensive employee opinion study. Every employee had been asked to complete a detailed questionnaire. Their comments, evaluations, and recommendations had been compiled into 26 volumes. Management, engrossed in business activities, had difficulty digesting all this material and knowing what to do with all the information.

The first approach to the research of professional suicide was a survey of individual effectiveness. It was important for the researcher to orient himself to the organization and become acquainted with the people, to open up avenues of communication, and to see if some of the recommendations of the employee opinion study could be put into effect by the people themselves rather than waiting for management to do it.

Approximately 180 people (mostly managers and engineers), received at least one interview, approximately two hours long, focusing on the ways in which they felt their usefulness to the organization might be increased. The results revealed that:

1. Most people were interested in doing a good job and wanted to be "committed," but frequently were confused about how to go about it.

2. A large number of those interviewed commented on the absence of performance reviews; that is, official management inputs relating to their performance and how it might be improved. (The absence of clearly stated and agreed-upon organizational goals had resulted in performance reviews becoming an evaluation of the individual's personality characteristics rather than an evaluation of organizational results achieved. This may partly explain why performance reviews had been largely discontinued.)

3. Some were reluctant to discuss personal problems, job-related problems, and organizational frustrations because of the importance placed on maintaining a positive public image. There was also reluctance to discuss problems because other interviews had been fed back to management by personnel people, and there was little belief in the personnel department's professional integrity. Fortunately, management agreed to the principle of confidentiality for this project, and this was a tremendous help in gaining acceptance by those who felt prior interviews with them had not been helpful.

4. Although there was resistance to an outsider investigating the operation of some departments, acceptance of the program by the organization was quite good. This was partly due to a general recognition throughout the organization of the importance of increasing people's effectiveness if the organization was to grow and prosper.

Phase II

Phase II was an individual psychotherapeutic treatment phase during which managers and engineers with problems were seen individually. Management's original approach to the problem was a humanitarian expression of concern for individuals involved in the suicide process. Implicit in this concern seemed to be the assumption that organizational problems were essentially individuals' problems.

It was noted very early in the study that there was a tendency on the part of management people to analyze organizational problems in terms of individual personality difficulties rather than in terms of interpersonal, group, intergroup or system problems. An obvious advantage of this approach, as seen by employees, was that a problem individual could be quickly identified and removed without the need for any organizational change other than fixing blame on this individual. Such procedure also allayed the anxiety created by vague, poorly defined fears, making it possible to pretend that what was wrong was known, and it was either minor or someone else's responsibility.

It soon became apparent that some of the people who tended to commit professional suicide were superior individuals, highly intelligent and committed (originally, at least), to improving the organization. Depth evaluations of these employees revealed little childhood pathology. A commonly held premise in clinics and social agencies is that if you look far enough you will find family pathology. However, it was not found in this group—perhaps because these were not typical clinic cases. In an industrial culture where one's future is dependent on a positive public image, it may be that these employees were just unwilling to reveal very much of themselves. But even when well known, they still appeared relatively free from childhood trauma and pathology. Their present difficulties could be traced largely to the highly stressful environment in which they found themselves. The findings of this study indicate that the pathology of these managers was more situational than psychological, and that their psychological reactions were primarily a result of prolonged situational stress.

The individual treatment approach of phase II proved very helpful to a number of managers and their families. It was found that some managers could be helped to change through working on emotional problems within their families when they were not willing to work on emotional problems at the job, even though both were symptomatic of the same basic difficulty. A wife or a child under stress provides more motivation for a manager to examine a need to change than does an employee under stress.

Because of the confidential nature of these activities, they had little organizational visibility. Also, their effect on the profit picture was not obvious enough for them to get the kind of organizational support needed to expand the effort beyond the demonstration stage.

Another problem encountered was the reluctance of managers, engineers, and scientists to accept what Satir calls the "medical-sickness model."[1] Although, for the most part, those involved in the process of professional suicide were aware they were in trouble, they were, by and large, unwilling to accept the traditional patient-client role (that is, the "50-minute hour," regular weekly interviews, and the other procedures that have become fairly standard within the mental health professions for providing help). If they had been fired, or if they had a very severe home problem, they would ask for help directly and accept a patient role, but usually not otherwise. It was important to their self-image and to their future organizational effectiveness that they see themselves and be seen by others as competent. Participating as a patient was not seen by them as being helpful with this. A significant step in the suicide process was coworkers or the personnel department convincing an individual that he had a problem. A commonly observed result of this "convincing" (in a highly competitive environment) was further deterioration and further progress toward professional suicide.

As a result, people much preferred to seek help in collaborative ways such as bull sessions of indeterminate length, usually outside office hours—either over lunch or in the evening. The swapping of articles and political points of view was a frequent opening ploy. Efforts to use the more traditional professional and mental health methods were largely unsuccessful. In this respect the project had to evolve techniques similar to those developed for working with street corner gangs.

Nevertheless, during the second year of the program, 128 individuals were seen with some 175 different problems. The majority of these individuals were managerial-supervisory people (67 managers-supervisors, 46 other salaried, 2 hourly, 13 spouses). The program was only publicized to managers-supervisors, partly for fear that one man would be swamped if the program became widely known. Nearly three-fifths of those seen were self referrals (74), the balance coming from bosses (18), personnel people (10), and friends (9). Problems were categorized as; those directly affecting work (boss-subordinate problems, severe job dissatisfaction, job confusion, very severe marital problems) (95); those only indirectly affecting work but of humanitarian concern (personality adjustment, marital, and parent-child problems) (35); and brief consultations on how to help others, career planning, requests for community resources, and so on (45).

Phase III

Phase III, which to some extent overlapped the first two phases, was an effort to influence the total psychological tone of the managerial environment of the organization. During phases I and II, it had become increasingly obvious that these bright young men were committing professional suicide because of certain pressures generated by the organizational climate. Among these perceived pressures were:

1. The problem of unclear, unrealistic expectations (the pressure of nebulous situations). Many managers were never quite clear where they stood with the organization and what was expected of them. Many were waiting for management to come up with answers while management was waiting for them to do the same.

2. A management philosophy of "running lean," which to some meant never enough resources to do the job right, but always enough to do it over. There was extensive use of "voluntary" overtime; 60- to 70-hour work weeks were not uncommon.

3. A management philosophy based on subordinate commitment, which was seen as meaning that advancement was based not so much on the job done (poorly defined at best), but on the effort and commitment demonstrated in doing it.

4. Poor planning and fatigue. When people are tired enough over a long enough period, they will respond only to crises. The result is that people are almost totally consumed in crisis interven-

tions and neglect orderly constructive efforts to reduce future crises.

5.   Poor communication and a special reluctance to advise people where they stand with respect to the scarcity of jobs within the organization. A lot of effort was directed toward placating people with platitudes that left them unaware regarding their job security.

6.   Because of the neglect (or fear) to communicate plans, people had gross misunderstandings of the organization, what it was trying to accomplish, and where they fit in as individuals.

7.   Too little recognition or even awareness of the good work being done, and a general preoccupation with problems past and present. This did little to strengthen individual confidence for the difficult tasks that needed doing.

8.   In several instances, great concern had been shown in keeping people happy, but at the expense of glossing over their problems for as long as possible and then resolving them by sudden transfer from one area to another. (This was done with praise, leaving the individual frustrated and the larger organization misled about what had really happened.)

9.   Emphasis for getting organizational tasks accomplished was placed on committed charismatic leaders who would get results with the use of minimal organizational resources. When such persons were found, they were in great demand, were given successively more difficult crises to solve (usually with only minimal opportunities for development and minimal formal organizational help) until they failed. When this occurred, their capabilities were reevaluated and eventually organizational hopes for success were transferred to new personalities.

10.   Although management pinned great hopes on committed charismatic leaders, their peers and the organization at large frequently saw them as threats. With organizational goals poorly defined, organizational relationships poorly communicated, and the authority to do a job largely withheld, it became more and more difficult for such leaders to obtain voluntary cooperation from peers already very busy with other things. If, in addition, organizational rewards seemed to be coming no closer and the joy

of task accomplishment was less frequent (either because of growing organizational resistance or mounting fatigue or both), it would seem unusual if some did not look for alternative uses for their energy.

With additional data it became increasingly evident that the problem was not so much the result of personality problems as it was an environmentally-culturally induced stress reaction. A strategy for coping more effectively with these difficulties might be found in working with groups of managers rather than just individuals. The purpose of these groups would be to reach more people than was possible through a one-by-one approach, to jointly explore improved means for increasing individual effectiveness as well as organizational effectiveness, to share pertinent information, to discover ways of influencing the psychological environment in a more positive direction, and to study the role of the leader in establishing a climate for effective task accomplishment.

To this end, interested managers were invited to attend groups that met once a week for about two hours. Using behavioral science teaching techniques of experiential learning rather than the more traditional academic lecture methods, these groups focused on improving one another's effectiveness and discussing how the effectiveness of the total organization might be improved.[2] They discussed managerial philosophy and administrative problems; but perhaps more important, these meetings provided a setting where managers could discuss their frustrations and disappointments in a neutral peer-group setting without being criticized for having a negative attitude.

These groups also experimented to see whether individual goals of increased effectiveness and improved understanding of the organization could be accomplished in the group without a group leader. The results of these group experiments were illuminating. We found that individuals were strengthened by belonging to a nonjudgmental peer group, but we also found that even groups of dedicated managers could not work effectively on a task without a leader to enforce persistence of effort (and to give rewards). The initial efforts on each new project were very enthusiastic, but over time other activities would become more and more interesting or demanding, and the original task would be neglected for want of leadership pressure. Or perhaps the lack of persistent effort was to keep any one of the leaders from being elevated in the group as a result of successful completion of a group project.

The members of these groups were originally regarded as emissaries of good management attitudes and practice who would return to their respective departments and institute management and organizational-environmental reforms for more effective task accomplishment. Unfortunately, the aspect of this company's management philosophy that said leaders could be influenced by subordinates was found not to apply with regard to subordinates' efforts to influence management philosophy. It appeared that most managers fail to exploit the managerial capabilities of their subordinates. Subordinates could develop more enlightened practices with *their* subordinates, but when it came to changing the behavior and attitudes of their superiors, subordinate attempts appeared to have little effect, and efforts in this direction usually resulted in even greater stress and frustration for the subordinates.

Phase IV

Phase IV emphasized team building. Because of the difficulties encountered in changing the total environmental culture by various individuals working alone, emphasis was altered from a focus on influencing the total organization to a focus on creating a more positive environment at the department level. In addition to working with individual problems of professional suicide, other kinds of mental health difficulties, and with groups of nonrelated managers, meetings were initiated in eight different departmental and functional areas to explore ways in which these organizational units could function more effectively. Through departmental meetings and the educational efforts of the department heads, an effort was made to develop and to build environments where the creative achievement drives of the project members could find greater expression than had been traditional. This had some success on an individual department basis.

Obviously the most important place where team building should be occurring is with the top man in the organization and his top team. Unless a philosophy of teamwork and team building is practiced at the top, it will be difficult to establish it lower down in the organization.[3] The second most important place where team building ought to be occurring is within the personnel department. As that department is responsible for assisting with the maintenance and development of effective human relations, it should be engaged in departmental team building if it is to help others build teams.

Phase V

In the summer of 1967, top management began to express concern about middle management's leadership capability. The symptoms leading up to this were a very close union election, declining profit margins, lowered morale, and the loss of a number of high-potential middle managers; and perhaps the concern came partly as a result of the grass roots educational efforts that had been going on. Problems were so general and widespread that middle management was unable to screen them any longer. It was difficult to hold any one individual responsible. As a result, the old human relations program was revitalized with the promise of more people to "walk, talk, and do," and a Christmas buffet for supervisory personnel was reinstituted.

A conclusion was also reached that something had to be done about improving salaried employee capability. An extensive evening education program was initiated to teach employees technical skills. Later, a manager development program was instituted, which used the concepts of T-group training to focus on improving managers' skills.

As a result of this latest development, the program entered phase V. This was an organization-wide cultural change, managerial development, organizational development program to build interpersonal competence and develop an environment where people would be strengthened for the difficult tasks that need to be done rather than deteriorating under pressure and becoming demoralized by them.

Greiner has pointed out that any kind of meaningful organizational change usually occurs only as a result of internal *and* external pressure for change. "Until the ground under top managers begins to shift, it seems unlikely that they will be sufficiently aroused to see the need for changes, both in themselves and in the rest of the organization."[4] Unless both internal and external pressures exist, it is easy for top management to excuse the pressure as temporary or inconsequential. As a result of the various pressures mentioned above, it may now be possible to apply the kinds of resources necessary to develop an environment where people can work effectively and creatively on organizational tasks and at the same time avoid professional suicide.

Implications

A number of studies have shown that mental health resources in the United States are too few and mental health problems too great to be influenced very soon through a one-by-one approach.[5] The value of an environmental-cultural milieu therapy approach to the correction and prevention of mental health problems has been demonstrated in mental hospitals, residential treatment centers, and residential schools,[6] but little has been done to apply these learnings and techniques on a community-wide basis, whether it be a geographical or an industrial community. The implications of this study for community mental health and the broad planning of prevention programs lie in demonstrating the value an environmental approach can have on improving human effectiveness and arresting human deterioration and professional suicide.

> It cannot be too strongly emphasized, since it is crucial in any planning for community health, that the social order, the institutional practices, and the whole array of customary patterns and relationships, the burdens and anxieties they impose, the persistent defeats and humiliation inflicted on people—these are all involved in the production of mental illness and must be taken into account in any attempt to promote healthy personalities.[7]

Notes

1. Virginia Satir, *Conjoint Family Therapy* (Palo Alto: Science and Behavioral Books, Inc., 1964).

2.   Leland Bradford, Kenneth Benne, and Jack Gibb, *T-Group Theory and Laboratory Method: Innovation in Education* (New York: Wiley, 1964).

3.   Robert J. House, *Management Development, Design, Evaluation and Implementation* (Ann Arbor: Bureau of Industrial Relations), 1967.

4.   Larry E. Greiner, "Patterns of Organizational Change," *Harvard Business Review,* May–June 1967, p. 126.

5.   George W. Albee, *Mental Health Manpower Trends* (New York: Basic Books) and Joint Commission on Mental Illness and Health, *Action for Mental Health* (New York: Science Editions, Inc., 1961).

6.   Milton Greenblat, Richard H. York, and Esther Lucile Brown, *From Custodial to Therapeutic Patient Care in Mental Hospitals* (New York: Russell Sage, 1955); Alfred H. Stanton and Morris S. Schwartz, *Mental Hospital* (New York: Basic Books, 1954); Bruno Bettelheim, *Love Is Not Enough* (New York: Free Press, 1950); A. S. Neill, *Summerhill* (New York: Hart Publishing Company, 1964).

7.   Lawrence K. Frank, "The Promotion of Mental Health," *Mental Health in the United States,* The Annals of the American Academy of Political and Social Science, vol. 286, March 1963, p. 169.

Creative Talent and Its Characteristics

I. Definitions of creativity

"The ability to produce repeatedly new results with new means."

"Creativity in the individual, regardless of intelligence, is a result of the lack of the normal instinct to mimic existing cultural patterns . . . We have been looking for the presence of something that does not exist instead of looking for the absence of something that does exist. Psychology should be able to measure the strength of the instinct to mimic." (6)

Three kinds of creativity:

1. ". . . The creation is clearly an expression of the inner states of the creator." e.g., novelists, essayists and poets.

2. "The creator acts largely to meet externally defined needs and goals. He produces a cordial and appropriate product but he adds little of himself to the result." e.g., industrial, researchers, engineers, scientists and mathematicians.

3. ". . . cuts across the other two in that the product is both an expression of the creator (thus very personal), and at the same time meets the demands of some external problem." e.g., architects. (7)

II. Theory (Two hypotheses by Max Beery of Seattle)

1. "There is no real correlation between intelligence and creativity. The apparent correlation is caused by

the fact that the higher the intelligence at a given creativity level, the more outstanding the result of that creativity. This phenomenon is accentuated by the tendency of the ability to communicate to be proportional to intelligence." (6)

2. "Knowledge is passed on from one generation to the next by three methods: inheritance of specific behavior patterns, training of the young, or through inheritance of a general behavior pattern or instinct to mimic the existing cultural pattern (tradition). The first is almost impossible to change because it is so complex and requires mutations for changes. The second depends upon the knowledge and ability of the elder to teach and the younger to learn, but behavior changes can occur without genetic changes—cultural evolution is possible. The third is our method, and seemingly an evolutionary improvement that is very efficient. Genetically speaking it is relatively young . . . logic is normally powerless against tradition, but some churches, lodges and philosophies have unwittingly developed tradition techniques—and seemed to develop a little traditional control. Mr. Beery feels that if a nation could learn to stop, start and control traditional behavior functions, it could rule the world." (6)

III. Characteristics of creativity

1. Intelligence

   a. After study of the top 20 percent of two types of students in a sample of 500, the "highly intelligent" and the "highly creative" (but not those who were high in both—now being studied further), two educational psychologists at the University of Chicago, Jacob W. Getzels and Philip W. Jackson, conclude:

     1. Emphasis on sense of humor is so marked among the creative group that it sets them sharply apart.

     2. High I.Q. children seek now the qualities that

they believe mean adult success. Creative children are not impressed by this goal.

3. High I.Q. children hew to a self-ideal they feel that teachers will approve. The creative child does not.

"In simple terms, the high I.Q. children tend to be conventional, to seek success in the standard known way, while the highly creative children diverge from the stereotype, seek to integrate fantasy and reality, enjoy the risk of seeking success through the unknown." (6)

b. ". . . Creative people as people . . . are fairly intelligent, but beyond this requirement, intelligence does not crucially determine the level of an individual's creativity." (7)

c. ". . . Most creative people are neither the most intelligent nor the grade-setters. As a result of spotty academic records, many are refused admission to graduate schools and are bypassed by companies looking for top-notch research men. Although a certain amount of intelligence is required for creativity—perhaps an I.Q. of 120— beyond that point it makes no difference. One factor that may keep many from being straight "A" students is their independence; they do well in subjects they like, but tend to neglect others they regard as unimportant." (4)

2. Age

a. "Early in life, creative individuals show the skills necessary to their ultimate careers, but many creative people come to their final careers late because they have so many skills and aptitudes that they find it difficult to choose among them." (7)

b. "In many cases 'creativity' has been linked with a youthful age group. This without hesitation, can be called pure assumption. Two factors are needed to actuate creativity; first and basically the 'talent,' and secondly the 'environmental condition.' The younger man with the talent can take the chance with a creative failure, the older one with greater sense of responsibility cannot. Relieved from such personal risk, the retired engineer who originally had the talent, again becomes a productive innovator." (6)

c. "Older persons tend to produce fewer solutions on the Power Source Apparatus Test, but to produce a larger saturation of workable solutions within those given. One might speculate that, with age, one learns what will *not* work." (5)

3. Interest in skills of creative people

a. "All score high on interests which might lead them to be psychologists, architects and authors. All score low on skills for purchasing agents, office workers, bankers, farmers, carpenters, policemen and morticians." (7)

4. Detail

a. "The signs are that creative talent is not very interested in small detail, in the practical and concrete, but is more concerned with the meanings, implications and symbolic equivalents of things and ideas." (7)

b. "Also, they seem to have a positive preference for complexity, even for what appears as disorder. Given a series of drawings of various types, they consistently choose those that are more abstract, perhaps chaotic; offered a choice to make mosaic patterns, the highly-creative tend to employ more colors, the less-creative fewer. It seems that the less-creative person has to impose order immediately, but the more creative sees the possibility of imposing a higher level of order." (7)

c. "Creative people prefer elegant solutions to problems. A classic example is the mathematician who ignores the obvious answer to a problem in order to arrive at a solution which he considers more sophisticated." (4)

5. Values of creative people

a. ". . . Creative people share the same values.

Spranger described the six basic values of men as being the esthetic, economic, political, social, religious and theoretical. For all creative types, the esthetic and theoretical are strongest; the economic tends to be weakest. The surprising thing is that esthetic and theoretical are supposed to be conflicting values, yet are of nearly the same strength in all creative groups. This suggests that creative people are able to tolerate the inner tensions created by holding conflicting values, or perhaps that they are able to resolve the conflict. Other findings support the hypothesis that creative individuals are more able to express opposite sides of their nature, to reconcile conscious and unconscious, reason and passion, rational and irrational, science and art." (7)

   b. "Actually, the creative person is the victim of the sharp conflict of values in our society today. We emphasize integration of the individual into the group and still try to nurture creative talent. These goals are fundamentally incompatible." (7)

6. Masculinity-femininity

   a. "All highly creative males . . . scored high on a 'femininity' test; they were more open in their feelings and emotions, more sensitively aware of themselves than others and possessed widely-ranging interests—traits which in our culture are considered feminine. On the other hand, most of them were not effeminate in manner and appearance, but instead, assertive, dominant and self-confident." (7)

7. Intuitiveness

   a. "Jung pointed out that when you think you either become aware of something (perceive), or come to a conclusion about something (judge). Most mathematicians, engineers and research scientists prefer the judging attitude. Among writers the preference is strongly reversed; about 80% are perceptives. Jung further subdivides perception into sense-perception—becoming aware of things directly by way of the senses, and intuitive-perception, which is indirect perception with a deeper meaning and an awareness of possibilities inherent in things. Three out of four of the general population are sense-perceptives. They concentrate on things presented to the five senses and focus their attention upon existing facts. The other one looks expectantly for a link between something present and something not yet thought of, focusing habitually upon possibilities. Highly creative people in all fields are overwhelmingly intuitive: 93% of the writers, 90% of the engineers and scientists, 100% of the architects." (7)

8. Conformity

   a. "The creative person is almost by definition not a conformist. His nonconformity lies in the realm of ideas, however, not necessarily of behavior. He is not usually emotionally unstable, sloppy, loose-jointed, Bohemian; he is simply independent." (7)

   b. "Although they are nonconformists in the realm of ideas, in social behavior they tend to be like everyone else. They often reflect what IPAR researchers call 'the briefcase syndrome': an outward appearance that makes them indistinguishable from ordinary businessmen. This makes the task all the more difficult for company recruiters who are looking for tell-tale signs." (4)

   c. "As judgment develops, imagination declines. Why? Imagination could conceivably parallel judgment—but doesn't. Or are they incompatible?" (8)

   d. "The ever-popular myth about the 'mad genius' has been proved fallacious by IPAR research. Although some of the creative geniuses in history have apparently had more mental problems than average, the IPAR groups have shown more ability than the average man to handle whatever complexes they may have. Even those who have a turbulent personality have a good ego mechanism to control it." (4)

9. Childhood

   a. "Creative people claim more than others do that their childhoods were not entirely happy. (This may be true or they may just be aware of things which others repress.) At any rate, the finding should not be interpreted by parents as meaning that they should make their children miserable in the hope of making them creative. It does mean, however, that parents should not force too much 'togetherness', that they should not prevent the child from turning in on himself. Efforts to produce 'well-rounded children' made often by both parents and schools, do not help creativity." (7)

   b. "Environment evidently plays some role in producing creative people. The most creative generally come from families that were not as close and loving as those of the less creative. When there is a distance between child and parent, the child has an opportunity to explore and develop at his own pace." (4)

   c. Those who reported that their family's income when they were 10–12 years old was about $3,000 a year tended to score significantly higher with respect to both creativity and productivity than those who reported either higher or lower incomes. These were essentially middle-income families. (9)

10. As students

    a. "Often the creative person is not a satisfactory student. He resists group work. He may set himself goals in conflict with those set for the class. He wants to follow his own interests." (7)

11. Work

    a. "In the realm of work, the creative say they find their jobs refreshing and never drudgery. They have a high level of energy, work long hours, seem less in need of vacations than their less-creative fellows. Thus, personnel policies built around a time-clock philosophy can be detrimental to creativity. Time has little meaning for the creative individual, who sometimes may appear to do nothing at all, and at other times may work for 24 hours without stopping." (4)

b. "Creative and uncreative individuals can work together, but do so poorly; the creative man likes to work alone and as he wills, not in a group and on schedule. Many employers are now recognizing this in various ways; they are separating research and engineering, or varying the organization diagram. The best plan seems to be to separate highly-creative individuals as far as possible physically from their noncreative counterparts, then put them on their mettle rather than on rules. And it's important to distinguish between true creativity—an idea that leads to something practical and marketable—and the 'idea man' who never gets anything practical done. The second one may be just a costly fad." (8)

c. "He found that more-creative men are more autonomous and dynamic, and at the same time less anxious than the less-creative. The more-creative have fewer authoritarian attitudes and give greater weight to the esthetic . . . The creative man seems to know when to be disciplined and when not. He is more likely to 'play', in a sense, with things and ideas. He is willing to allow all kinds of ideas and feelings to enter his mind. Highly creative men do not attack a problem as most of us do. They tend to become part of the problem itself, sensing its forces and following its leads; thus, they let the problem solve itself. The less-creative workers seem more oriented toward quick achievement; the more creative ones work slowly at work marshaling resources, then they work quickly and certainly to a synthesis. The less creative try to achieve the synthesis earlier, then keep checking back, retracing steps." (7)

d. ". . . Scientists are more creative when they are slightly uncomfortable. They need to be jarred by the unexpected, forced to an unusual or creative response by a condition of intellectual uncertainty or 'dither.' Anxiety, on the other hand, seems to inhibit creativity. What is needed is enough uncertainty to stimulate innovation, but enough security to offset anxiety that uncertainty arouses. Maximum creativity should thus be found in situations containing both high dither and high security." (7)

e. ". . . I believe that the creative individual not only respects the irrational in himself, but courts it as the most promising source of novelty in his own thinking. When such admissibility is granted to the ordinarily tabooed thoughts and impulses which have undergone an earlier repression in the interests of immediate adaptation, the individual may at times appear to others to be unbalanced. The unbalance which comes about in such a fashion is, however, according to my view, essentially integrative and as such is health-tending." (1)

12. Results of the research scientists—Q-Sort deck

a. "The Q-Sort Deck consists of 56 cards, each with a descriptive phrase such as 'indifferent to the practical applications of his own research', or 'is good at developing work-saving ideas and approximation techniques.' " (4)

b. "Each researcher in the IPAR group was asked to sort these cards into five self-descriptive groups with each group rated according to its importance. After the results of this self-analysis were correlated with other tests, eight stylistic types were isolated. These were called: the zealot, initiator, diagnostician, scholar, artificer, aesthetician, methodologist, independent. Based on previous scores of creative originality, the zealot shows the greatest creative potential, followed closely by the methodologist. The artificer and independent scored low as innovators. The zealot is dedicated to research; he sees himself as a driving, indefatigable research man, with exceptional mathematics skills and a lively sense of curiosity. Others see him as tolerant and conscientious, but not getting along easily with others or 'fitting in.' The artificer, at the other end of the scale, gives freely of his time and enjoys talking shop with other researchers. Aware of his limitations, he does not attempt what he cannot do. He sees himself as having a special facility for taking poorly formed ideas of others and working them into significant programs. His colleagues see him as direct, honest and getting along well with people." (4)

13. Development of creativity

"A very good way to make a horse balky is to try at the very beginning to make him pull more than he thinks he can . . . The best way to make outstanding creative persons is to make good hacks— I mean, people who just keep working—because it seems to me that the creative things always come out of, along with, and incidental to, a lot of things that are sometimes not even good." (3)

14. Summary

". . . Creative people, no matter what their profession, tend to have the same interests and characteristics. They are, in general, bright, independent, curious, skeptical of accepted ideas, dedicated to their work, intuitive, open to experience, and aesthetically sensitive." (4)

IV. Problems

1. "Science has done its utmost to prevent whatever science has done."—Sir William Gilbert (1540–1603). (8)

2. "Organizations need a defense against innovators. They set up forces to keep out ideas simply because

the organization would dissolve in chaos if all suggested—and good—changes were made. This is true of both government and of industry; they resist ideas while begging for them." (6)

3. "Even within an organization, it is hard to get a hearing for ideas. The martyrdom—either on the part of the innovator or on the part of a dedicated sponsor (e.g., Admiral Rickover) is essential . . . In the usual instance the innovator or his sponsor needs the help of an Archimedes—a place outside the 'world'—on which to stand and get added leverage. The footrest can be the Congress or the President in the case of government, or the public in the case of a company. If enough leverage can be applied through these, the idea has at least a chance to be considered with some likelihood of acceptance." (6)

4. "There is a very real conflict between the concepts of creativity and sound management. Creativity demands the sacrifice of everything else to ideas; management demands a devotion to conformity, to solidity and solidarity as a way of generating and enhancing profit. Change creates an unsettled atmosphere, high costs, problems. All these upset management. But stop change and you have a rigor that soon leads to rigor mortis." (8)

5. "Any outstanding advance in science or engineering requires an 'essential tension' between an orientation toward tradition or wisdom and one directed toward innovation or novelty. Thomas S. Kuhn points out that if society emphasizes wisdom and novelty, the highest results are achieved. This is, in general, an unlikely combination. It has occurred broadly only twice in our history, the first time in Athens in the fourth century before Christ, the second time during the Renaissance. Sparta was too moral, China too contemplative, Egypt too religious to attain full creativity; there must be an atmosphere of concentration on the future, not on the past, on the individual's output rather than on the way he lives. We are currently too

imbued with the 'fuller life' to place necessary emphasis on advance. We tend to appreciate convergent, rather than divergent, thinking." (8)

6. "It is essential to achieve two things if we are to recognize our national creative potential. One is to teach more professional people how to use their creativity effectively, the other is to make creativity more acceptable socially, thus to enhance the motivations." (8)

7. ". . . The individual in our society who does have an aggressive problem-solving orientation is often considered ill-mannered. And as everyone knows, it is much easier to bear the stigma of immorality than of bad manners! The problem solver is unquestionably a deviant, and making good use of him is one of the major challenges of our society. A revealing experiment on this has been devised by Shepard. He gave a problem to a series of groups created for the purposes of the experiment. Some of these groups contained a 'deviant', others did not. In every case, the group containing a deviant came out with a richer analysis of the problem and a more elegant solution. The next step was to request each group to throw out one member. The deviant was thrown out every time! As long as the group had to work with him the results were creative, but faced with a choice the group found it easier to continue minus the person who forced them to confront conflicting views and integrate them." (2)

To Deal with Organizational Conflict

"There are many possible approaches, and most of them have already been touched upon. Sometimes a structural change is indicated, sometimes individual therapy is indicated, and many gradations of approaches lie in between. The best organizational lubricant will probably always be an ability on the part of each individual to accept the others as they are.

Many tensions and difficulties become manageable in a setting of mutual acceptance and emotional security which would rip a more hostile and defensive group wide open." (2)

Notes

1. Barron, Frank. "The Need for Order and Disorder as Motives in Creative Activity," *The Second University of Utah Research Conference on Identification of Creative Scientific Talent* (Salt Lake City: University of Utah Press, 1958), p. 122.

2. Boulding, Elsie. *Conflict Management in Organizations* (Ann Arbor: Foundation for Research on Human Behavior, 1961), pp. 54–56.

3. Eyring, Henry. "Scientific Creativity," *The Second University of Utah Research Conference on Identification of Creative Scientific Talent* (Salt Lake City: University of Utah Press, 1958), p. 156.

4. Keene, Jenness. "How to Spot Creative Talent," *Chemical Engineering,* June 25, 1962, pp. 136–138.

5. Owens, W. A., Schumacher, C. F., and Clark, J. B. "The Measurement of Creativity in Machine Design," *The Second University of Utah Research Conference on the Identification of Creative Scientific Talent* (Salt Lake City: University of Utah Press, 1958), p. 140.

6. Tangerman, E. J. "Creativity . . . A New Appraisal," *Product Engineering,* XXXI, Dec. 12, 1960, pp. 79–81.

7. Tangerman, E. J. "Creativity: What Is It?", *Product Engineering,* XXXII, Dec. 11, 1961, pp. 63–65.

8. Tangerman, E. J. "Today's Creativity," *Product Engineering,* Sept. 16, 1963, pp. 105–107.

9. Taylor, Calvin W., Principal Investigator. *The Second University of Utah Research Conference on Identification of Scientific Talent* (Salt Lake City: University of Utah Press, 1958).

The "Brownie Point" System: A Study of an Organization's Perceived and Ideal Reward Systems

Introduction

For individuals to use themselves appropriately and helpfully in the accomplishment of organizational tasks, it is necessary that they understand the goals and the values of the situation in which they find themselves. In any group endeavor, it is important that the individuals involved understand their common purpose and each other so that their activity can advance group purpose instead of resulting in canceling out one another's efforts. The degree to which group purpose and values are cloudy and unclear is the degree to which those interested in achieving a group purpose will have difficulty. If it can be demonstrated that a group of people, supposedly working in a common effort toward a common goal, are not in agreement on the objective or on the value system within which they are operating, then it is likely that maximum cooperation and utilization of the available skills and talents are not being achieved.

This study began at the bar during a banquet rewarding long-time employees. Someone asked, "What does it take to get ahead in this company?" Disagreement started almost immediately about what employee behavior was rewarded and what was censured. There was general agreement that a "brownie point" system did exist, and that some behavior was rewarded with plus points and other behavior was punished with minus points. But there was relatively little agreement on what behavior added points and what behavior subtracted points, let alone any agreement on how many points. The study of an organizational reward system was conducted among a nonhomogeneous grouping of employees, all of whom worked in one department, all reporting to the same boss (or whose bosses reported to the same boss). It comprised 14 people—a 100 percent sample (except for the writer) of a departmental work group that had been meeting weekly for several months with regard to common functional tasks.

Employee Perceptions of the Department's Present "Brownie Point" System

In consultation with department members, a questionnaire was constructed describing 20 different kinds of behavior (see Table C-1, page 207). In column 1, employees were asked to state the number of points (from $+10$ through 0 to -10) that they felt from their experience they would earn at the present time (from their boss or from a larger system) for each of the items of behavior listed. For example, if they felt being a "yes man" was important to the organization, then they would list perhaps $+10$, or $+9$ in column I. If they felt that being a "yes man" was of negative importance, then they might list -1, or -2, to -10, and so on.

As expected, there was little agreement about whether some items were rewarded or punished. For example, the number of points respondents thought would be given for question 14, "Getting someone fired"; question 1, "Being a 'yes man' (always agreeing with your boss)"; question 15, "Civic activities (YMCA and Boy Scouts)" ranged from $+10$ points to -10—the widest range possible. Only one question, 11, had less than a 10-point difference between the answers given by various members of the departments. On only two questions, 16 and 20, was there unanimous agreement that plus points were rewarded for this behavior. On half of the items there was disagreement about whether a specific behavior would receive plus points or minus points.

Behavior that on the average was seen as being most strongly rewarded in the present system was 4, "Initiate any new program 'all on your own' "; 5, "Participation in the initiation of a new program (part of a team effort)"; and 20, "Doing a job well, on time, and in completed form." These three activities each received a median score of +5 "brownie points." Behavior seen as being most punished by the present system was 1, "Being a 'yes man' (always agreeing with your boss)"; and 10, "Refusing to give to the United Appeal or Good Government." Each received a median of −5 brownie points.

Opinions on the Ideal System

In column 2, respondents were asked to state the number of points (from +10 through 0 to −10) that they felt the organization *should* award for each of the different items of behavior listed at the left. There was more agreement among respondents on the ideal system than there was on how they perceived the present situation. (The range of points in the ideal system averaged 11 per item, while points given to behavior in the present system ranged an average of 13 per item.) The greatest range of disagreement on how many points should be given in the ideal system was number 2, "Getting into big trouble requiring lots of help," where answers ranged from +10 to −5; number 6, "Glad-handing it, spending time being sociable and pleasant to lots of people," where answers also ranged from +10 to −5; and number 7, "Working at least 60 hours a week," where answers ranged from +6 to −10.

That behavior that employees felt should have the most brownie points in the ideal system was number 16, "Being creative—technically innovative," with a median score of +10 points. Interestingly, number 8, "Doing a good job in a quiet manner with little fanfare and without getting into any big difficulties"; and number 20, "Doing a job well, on time, and in completed form," received a median of only +8 points. That behavior which employees thought should receive the most negative points (and this was by considerable margin) was number 1, "Being a 'yes man' (always agreeing with your boss)," with a median of −9 points. The high negative score that people felt should be attached to always agreeing with your boss might explain to some extent why it was relatively difficult to get agreement within this working group.

Organizational Dissonance

The difference between the number of points employees felt were rewarded within the present system and the number of points they felt *should* be rewarded within an ideal system can be defined as organizational dissonance. Essentially, organizational dissonance is the lack of agreement between what people think the present system is and what they feel it should be. This lack of agreement might also be defined as the extent to which an organization is sick, or out of phase with what people feel ought to be. The greatest organizational dissonance occurred in 8, "Doing a good job in a quiet manner with little fanfare and without getting into any difficulty." The mean difference between what people felt the present system actually awarded and the ideal system should award was almost 5 points. Other activities for which the actual reward was thought to differ most severely from the ideal reward were 18, "Developing and training subordinates," with a mean difference between the actual and the ideal of 4.3 points; and 10, "Refusing to give to the United Appeal or Good Government," with a mean difference of 4.2 points. Respondents thought more credit should be given for developing and training of subordinates, and fewer points should be subtracted for not giving to Good Government than they believed was the actual case.

There was a wide range between individuals in the way they saw the existing system when contrasted with their ideal systems. The mean organizational dissonance (that is, the difference that individuals felt existed between their perception of the current value system and their own ideal reward systems) ranged from 0 to 5.86 points per item. In other words, one person in the department saw no difference between the actual point system and his ideal system, whereas another individual saw an average difference of 5.86 points per item between his view of the existing system and how he would award points in an ideal system. The difference between the actual point system and the ideal system for all individuals averaged 3.5 points per item. Although there is no standard for comparison, a difference averaging out to 3.5 points per item between what the existing system rewards and what people think the ideal system should award seems high.

The Leader's Ideal System

The leader of the group was asked to state the number of points he thought should be awarded to various kinds of behavior in his ideal system. There was little difference from the medians of what the group felt should be awarded in an ideal system. Variation was within one point, except for two items. On item 1, "Being a 'yes man' (always agreeing with your boss)," the leader felt this behavior should receive no points, whereas the median for the group was -9. This is quite a difference and reflects a serious lack of group understanding about what the leader regards as ideal behavior. Such a strongly held negative value could account for the lack of cooperation in the group, with resulting leadership problems. The group obviously assigned a very negative value to being a yes man, while the leader felt it was of no negative consequence. As a result, individuals probably strove actively not to always agree with the leader, with resulting problems in group cooperation.

The other item of greatest disagreement between the ideal systems of the group and the leader was 7, "Working at least 60 hours a week." The median for the group indicated that in the ideal system this should receive no points, while the leader felt it should receive -5 points. Obviously, the leader felt more negative about working at least 60 hours a week than did the group. Publication of the leader's evaluation of these kinds of behavior might have resulted in a better understanding of what the leader values and greater agreement from individuals who do not have strong personal needs for continuing behavior which is not particularly appreciated.

Organizational dissonance with reference to the leader averaged 2.35 points per item, somewhat less than the median organizational dissonance for the group, 3.5 points per item. This indicated that the leader was more in tune with the organization than was the group as a whole. One would expect that he, as leader, would perceive the actual operation of the system as more positive (closer to his ideal system) than would group members, who deal more intimately with the system and who may be more aware of its limitations and problems.

Problems in the Study

There were some problems in the structure and presentation of the questionnaire which might have made the results less precise than desired:

1. The questions might have been more carefully worded. Some of the differences obtained between people may be because not everyone understood the questions in the same way.

2. Because individuals were interviewed personally, they might have given more uniform answers than if they had been free to answer anonymously.

3. While the concept of the brownie point system seemed to offer no particular difficulty, the range of points did. People were restricted to rewarding a kind of behavior with no more than 10 points and penalizing no more than -10. This obviously created some problems. Some people had difficulty in deciding just how many plus points and just how many minus points should be awarded. If this study contained only differences in the degree to which a behavior was plus or minus, it would not be as significant. Of greater significance was that wide variations were found in whether a certain kind of behavior was plus or minus.

4. There was some difficulty in the instructions in that it was not always clear from which reward system the individual should answer. Line personnel people, especially, operate within several different reward systems (the personnel department, the line organization, and the larger corporate structure), all of which may vary with regard to behavior rewarded or penalized. However, the existence of so many different reward systems is an organizational problem in itself to which a group personnel department might someday want to address itself.

5. Some people had difficulty because they could not respond to a question relating to behavior without knowing intent. Because this was a large organization where intent was often difficult to know and where intentions behind actions are interpreted very differently by different people, items were designed to include only the actual behavior itself, with intent omitted. While this created problems for some respondents, it seemed a more valid way to conduct the study.

Summary

A study of the brownie point system was conducted in one department of a large corporation to determine to what extent individuals agreed on the reward system then in effect, to what extent they agreed on an ideal reward system, and to what extent they saw the existing reward system as differing from the ideal system. This study found little general agreement among respondents on their perception of the existing reward system. For people to function effectively together, there should be greater consensus on what the organization rewards and does not reward.

Interestingly, there seemed to be greater consensus on what the system should be than on what the system was. Even here, however, there was considerable lack of agreement. While lack of agreement may have been related to differences in understanding specific questions, the fact that there was general agreement between the group mean and the leader's answers would seem to indicate that there was not so much the lack of understanding of the question as there was much disagreement between individuals on desired behavior. A discussion of desired behavior by the members of this group (with the leader present) would probably do much to create a greater unanimity of opinion and more cooperative behavior.

One measure of organizational illness is the degree to which the ideal system differs from the existing system. The difference between individual's scores on the actual system when contrasted with the ideal system ranged from no difference to a difference of 5.86 points per item. A mean difference per individual of 3.5 points per item seems to indicate that most saw quite a difference between the reward system in practice and what they thought should be in practice. Because of the extent to which the personnel department could influence the organizational reward system (for example, by raises and promotions), it seemed to be in a uniquely advantageous position to move the organization toward a more ideal system. The desirability of the personnel department being in greater agreement on an ideal system appeared obvious if the organization was to move ahead smoothly and efficiently.

The lack of agreement between the ideal system of the leader and the ideal system of the group on 1, "Being a 'yes man' (always agreeing with your boss)," and 7, "Working at least 60 hours a week," may have been related to the lack of cooperation that existed between members of the department and to the tendency toward working long hours.

It was recommended that at some time the leader discuss at greater length with his group what he regarded as desirable behavior from them. They would, obviously, have been more likely to exhibit the kind of behavior he desired, if they had known what kind of behavior he favored and what kind he disfavored. As the person who ultimately dispenses organizational favors, the leader is in control of the reward system and can use these favors and control of the reward system in many ways to elicit organizationally desirable behavior.

Table C-1   An Attempt to Specify the "Brownie Point" System

On this page are listed a number of different kinds of behavior. In column 1, please state the number of points (from $+10$ through 0 to -10) that you feel from your experience here you would earn at the present time (from your boss or from the larger system) for each of the items of behavior listed on the left. For example, if you feel being a "yes man" is important to the organization, then you would list perhaps $+10$, $+9$, etc., in column 1. If you feel that being a "yes man" is immaterial, then you might list 0 in column 1. If you feel being a "yes man" is of negative importance, then you might list -1, -2, etc.

In column 2, please state the number of points (from $+10$ to -10) that you feel the organization *should* award for each of the different items of behavior listed at the left.

	Column 1	Column 2
	Present Point System	The Ideal System
1. Being a "yes man" (always agreeing with your boss)	___	___
2. Getting into big trouble requiring lots of help	___	___
3. Social contacts (lunches, playing golf, etc.)	___	___
4. Initiating any new program "all on your own"	___	___
5. Participating in the initiation of a new program (part of a team effort)	___	___
6. Glad-handing it. Spending time being sociable and pleasant to lots of people	___	___
7. Working at least 60 hours a week	___	___
8. Doing a good job in a quiet manner with little fanfare and without getting into any big difficulties	___	___
9. Giving to United Appeal or Good Government	___	___
10. Refusing to give to United Appeal or Good Government	___	___
11. Getting *one* person upset as a result of trying to do a good job	___	___
12. Getting *two* people upset as a result of trying to do a good job	___	___

Table C-1 An Attempt to Specify the "Brownie Point" System
(Continued)

	Column 1	Column 2
	Present Point System	The Ideal System
13. Asking a question on any subject requiring a definite decision	_____	_____
14. Getting someone fired	_____	_____
15. Civic activities (YMCA, Boy Scouts)	_____	_____
16. Being creative—technically innovative	_____	_____
17. Participating in technical societies and writing papers	_____	_____
18. Developing and training subordinates	_____	_____
19. "Leveling"—Telling subordinates (in private and unemotionally) how they could improve their performance	_____	_____
20. Doing a job well, on time, and in completed form	_____	_____
Other behavior (for which points are given or subtracted)		
	_____	_____
	_____	_____
	_____	_____

Your name _____

Table C-2

Summary of an Attempt to Specify the Reward System	Column 1 Perceptions of the Present System		Column 2 Perceptions of the Ideal System		Difference between Present and Ideal System		Leader's Ideal System
	Range	Median	Range	Median	Range	Mean	
1. Being a "yes man" (always agreeing with your boss)	+10 to -10	-5	+2 to -10	-9	12 to 0	2.21	0
2. Getting into big trouble requiring lots of help	+5 to -7	-1.5	+5 to -10	-2	15 to 0	2.21	-1
3. Social contacts (lunches, playing golf, etc.)	+10 to -7	+4	+5 to 0	0	10 to 0	2.96	0
4. Initiating any new program "all on your own"	+10 to -1	+5	+10 to -5	+6	8 to 0	3.5	+5
5. Participating in the initiation of a new program (part of a team effort)	+10 to 0	+5	+10 to 0	+5	5 to 0	2.46	+5
6. Glad-handing it. Spending time being sociable and pleasant to lots of people	+10 to 0	+4	+10 to -5	0	10 to 0	3.53	0
7. Working at least 60 hours a week	+10 to 0	+2	+6 to -10	0	20 to 0	4	-5
8. Doing a good job in a quiet manner with little fanfare and without getting into any big difficulties	+10 to 0	+3	+10 to +3	+8	15 to 0	4.71	+7
9. Giving to United Appeal or Good Government	+10 to 0	+2	+5 to 0	0	10 to 0	1.85	0

Table C-2 *(Continued)*

Summary of an Attempt to Specify the Reward System	Column 1 Perceptions of the Present System		Column 2 Perceptions of the Ideal System		Difference between Present and Ideal System		Leader's Ideal System
	Range	Median	Range	Median	Range	Mean	
10. Refusing to give to United Appeal or Good Government	0 to −10	−5	+5 to −6	0	10 to 0	4.23	0
11. Getting *one* person upset as a result of trying to do a good job	+5 to −3.5	0	+3 to −3	0	5 to 0	1.75	0
12. Getting *two* people upset as a result of trying to do a good job	+5 to −5	−2	+5 to −2	0	7 to 0	2.5	−1
13. Asking a question on any subject requiring a definite decision	+10 to −6	0	+5 to 0	0	10 to 0	2.53	0
14. Getting someone fired	+10 to −10	0	0 to −10	0	10 to 0	2.2	0
15. Civic activities (YMCA, Boy Scouts)	+10 to −10	+4	+10 to 0	+3	12 to 0	2.69	+2
16. Being creative—technically innovative	+10 to +2	+5	+10 to +5	+10	7 to 0	3	
17. Participation in technical societies and writing papers	+10 to 0	+3	+10 to 0	+6	7 to 0	3.5	

18.	Developing and training subordinates	+10 to 0	+3	+10 to +4.5	+8	9 to 0	4.26	
19.	"Leveling"—telling subordinates (in private and unemotionally) how they could improve their performance	+10 to −2.5	+3	+10 to +2.5	+7	8 to 0	2.07	+5
20.	Doing a job well, on time, and in completed form	+10 to +3	+5	+10 to +5	+8	7 to 0	1.84	+10

Other behavior for which respondents thought points were given or subtracted:

Associating only with those at your level or higher	+8
Being unobtrusive—really staying out of sight	+7
Reporting "interesting interaction"	+7
Discussing performance objectively, yours or another's	−9
Guilty of poor judgment—timing	−5
Promotion of group-individual interaction	+2
Self improvement	0

+2
−7
−5
+8
−1
+8
+5

The "organizational dissonance" (i.e., the differences individuals felt existed between their perceptions of the existing value system and their own ideal value systems) ranged from 0 to 5.86 points per item. Organizational dissonance as seen by the members of the personnel department averaged 3.5 points per item.

The Manager's Dilemma: A Group Exercise on Competition/Cooperation

Most people are familiar with the so called prisoner's dilemma: Two men are captured following a crime. They are taken to separate rooms and interrogated. Under questioning, each man has to decide whether he will plead innocent or turn "state's evidence." If both plead innocent, they will both go free, for there is no evidence against them. However if A pleads innocent and B turns state's evidence, A will go to jail and B will be rewarded. If, on the other hand, A turns state's evidence and B maintains his innocence, A will be rewarded and B will go to jail. If both try to turn state's evidence, neither will be rewarded and both will be found guilty and go to jail. The dilemma each prisoner faces as to whether he should plead innocent or turn state's evidence is pictured in the diagram below with values assigned to each set of circumstances.

Businessmen face a somewhat similar dilemma. Almost daily, they must decide whether to compete in a self-enlightened gentlemanly way or whether to compete viciously. If businessmen compete with each other in a gentlemanly, non-cut-throat manner, they may get slightly higher prices for their products, while if they compete viciously, they may both go out of business. A can make the greatest gain if he competes viciously with B, while B competes only in a gentlemanly manner with A. The following table assigns arbitrary values to the advantages of gentlemanly or vicious competition.

The Prisoner's Dilemma

Prisoners Plead		Prisoner Receives	
A	B	A	B
Innocent	Innocent	Freedom ($+1$)	Freedom ($+1$)
Innocent	State's evidence	Severe sentence (-2)	freedom and reward ($+2$)
State's evidence	Innocent	Freedom and reward ($+2$)	Severe sentence (-2)
State's evidence	State's evidence	Jail (-1)	Jail (-1)

The Businessman's Dilemma

Businessman's Choice		Resulting Score	
A	B	A	B
Gentlemanly competition	Gentlemanly competition	$+1$	$+1$
Gentlemanly competition	Vicious competition	-2	$+2$
Vicious competition	Gentlemanly competition	$+2$	-2
Vicious competition	Vicious competition	-1	-1

In many organizations the ethics and philosophies of the competitive market place are moved into the business itself. Division heads and department heads are expected to compete with one another for facilities, personnel, and capital investment, as well as for the next higher job up the line. Organizing an operation with many profit centers and individual profit measurements encourages competition between organizational subgroups.

In daily decision making, the manager has to choose between a managerial stance of cooperation and team effort and an attitude of competition and individual entrepreneurship. The organization *may* recognize and reward cooperation; but successful competition not only makes the manager look good, but also makes rivals look bad. By competing, the manager will score twice as many points as by cooperating; and, in addition, points will be deducted from rivals' scores. If the rivalry becomes too open, however, and they compete too viciously, an impasse may result —in which case they will both lose points because both will fail.

For most organizations to fulfill their missions, the people within it must coordinate their efforts. Cooperation makes it possible to achieve results that an isolated individual would never be able to accomplish alone. The following chart illustrates this situation:

The Manager's Dilemma

Manager's Choice		Resulting Score	
A	B	A	B
Cooperate (Green)	Cooperate (Green)	+1	+1
Cooperate (Green)	Compete (Red)	−2	+2
Compete (Red)	Cooperate (Green)	+2	−2
Compete (Red)	Compete (Red)	−1	−1

A group exercise demonstrating the manager's dilemma can be conducted by dividing any group into teams of two. Each person on each team secretly chooses either red or green. Their score is then determined from the preceding chart. After this has been done several times, determine who got the highest score. How many times did the winner choose green? What is the ratio of green to red responses for the entire group?

When two people are told the scoring and then asked to secretly pick either red or green, it eventually becomes apparent that there are really only three strategies: unconditional cooperation (always choose green), conditional cooperation ("tit for tat," or "I'll treat you as you treat me"), and unconditional competition ("I'll try to get you every time"). In the game outlined above, with the values shown, it will usually work out that when played for an extended time, the most will be gained by making green, or cooperative, responses.

A crucial factor in determining how the game will be played are the values attached to the various alternatives. If the game were played with no points for cooperative behavior, one would obviously find relatively less cooperative behavior. In some companies, where performance reviews are not given, few objectives and goals exist, and competition between individuals is encouraged, employees may come to feel that few—if any—points are given for cooperating in doing a good job. A measurement system based solely on financial results (profits, return on investments, or contribution to earnings per share) tends to reward those who compete viciously and makes little allowance for the intangible effects of cooperation.

After the earlier game has been played, play the game again using the values listed below. After a number of turns, again determine who has won. How many times did the winner use green? What does this mean? Compare the total number of green responses in the first game with the total number of responses in the second game. What does this mean?

The Manager's Dilemma in Organizations Without Rewards for Cooperation

Manager's Choice		Resulting Score	
A	B	A	B
Green (cooperation)	Green (cooperation)	0	0
Green (cooperation)	Red (competition)	−2	+2
Red (competition)	Green (cooperation)	+2	−2
Red (competition)	Red (competition)	−1	−1

The solution to obtaining more cooperative responses from participants in the first game does not lie in modifying their personality characteristics, as the adherents of some management schools would urge. The answer lies in changing the value system of the organization so that a higher reward is given for results and cooperative behavior (assuming cooperation is, in fact, desired). A business can expect its managers to optimize their performance in accordance with the value system by which their performance is measured and rewarded. It is important for top management to realize that the system of rewards and penalties used in the organization strongly influences behavior, and managers cannot be expected to cooperate in the accomplishment of tasks if the organization's value system does not encourage cooperation. The establishment of a value system that rewards organizationally desired behavior, of course, presupposes that the keepers of the reward system know the kinds of behavior that are organizationally desired. Although the primary function of a manager in business is to make money through the accomplishment of organizational objectives, many present-day managers seem unable to define the objectives of their departments. Obviously, if managers cannot establish organizational objectives, it is difficult to establish a rational reward system.

Summary

This little game demonstrates that the behavior exhibited by members of an organization is not solely a function of the individual's personality adjustment, but is heavily influenced by and largely a function of the organization's and the boss's reward systems. Behavior that receives the highest and most consistent reward will be that behavior most commonly exhibited by people who are reality oriented. (There are some people who will continue to exhibit cooperative behavior even when it is not rewarded, but this would have to be labeled neurotic because it is not reality oriented.)

When performance is not evaluated formally but left to grapevine evaluation or gossip, employees are deprived of reliable data about their work. With no formal record being kept of their accomplishments, they may eventually come to feel that the company is not really interested in good work, but only in problems. As a result, they may spend more time in trying to make competitors look bad than in doing a good job themselves. An answer to this problem may be found by increasing the value given to desired behavior.

Bibliography

Adams, J. S., and Patricia R. Jacobsen. "Effects of Wage Inequality on Work Quality," *Journal of Abnormal and Social Psychology,* 69, 1964.

Albee, George W. *Mental Health Manpower Trends* (New York: Basic Books) and Joint Commission on Mental Illness and Health, *Action for Mental Health* (New York: Wiley, 1961).

Ammons, S. R. B. "Effects of Knowledge of Performance Survey and Tentative Theoretical Formulation," *Journal of General Psychology,* 1954.

Anderson, W. D. E., R. W. Quirk, et al. "Industrial Change, Challenge and Opportunity," *The Journal of Industrial Engineering,* vol. XVIII, no. 10, October 1967.

Argyris, Chris. *Organization and Innovation* (Homewood, Ill.: Irwin, 1965).

———. *Personality in Organization* (New York: Harper & Row, 1957).

———. "T-Groups for Organizational Effectiveness," *Harvard Business Review,* March–April 1964.

Arnold, William. "The Engineer and His Profession," *Product Engineering,* June 17, 1968, p. 130. Reporting on the findings of a three-year study at Stanford Research Institute by Howard M. Vollmer, to be called *Handbook of Organizational Design.*

Bennis, Warren G. *Changing Organizations* (New York: McGraw-Hill, 1966).

Berne, Eric. *Games People Play* (New York: Grove Press, 1964).

Bettelheim, Bruno. *Love Is Not Enough* (New York: Free Press, 1950).

Biderman, Albert D. "Life and Death in Extreme Captivity Situations," Bureau of Social Science Research, Washington, April 1967.

———. *Psychological Stress,* Mortimer H. Appley and Richard Trumbull (eds.) (New York: Appleton, 1967).

Blake, Robert, and Jane Mouton. *The Managerial Grid* (Houston: Gulf, 1964).

Boulding, Elsie. *Conflict Management in Organizations* (Ann Arbor: Foundation for Research on Human Behavior, 1961).

Bradford, Leland, Kenneth Benne, and Jack Gibb. *T-Group Theory and Laboratory Method: Innovation in Education* (New York: Wiley, 1964).

Brady, Joseph V. "Ulcers in Executive Monkeys," *Frontiers of Psychological Research* (San Francisco: Freeman, 1964).

Cofer, C. N., and M. H. Appley. *Motivation Theory and Research* (New York: Wiley, 1964).

Cole, Donald W. "The 'Brownie Point' System, A Study of an Organization's Perceived and Idealized Reward System," September 1965. (See App. C.)

———. "Evaluation of the Manager Development Program," August 1968.

Conn, L. K., and D. P. Crowne. "Instigation to Aggression, Emotional Arousal and Defense Emulation," *Journal of Personality,* 32, 1964.

Coogan, Joseph P. "Simian Society Research at Yerkes Primate Center," *SK&F Psychiatric Reporter,* 38, May–June 1968.

Conquest, Bob. "Community Mental Health," *Announcer,* Cleveland Psychological Association, vol. V, no. 2, January 1969.

Coopersmith, Stanley. "Studies in Self-Esteem," *Scientific American,* February 1968.

Cyert, R. M., and James G. March. *A Behavioral Theory of the Firm* (Englewood Cliffs, N.J.: Prentice-Hall, 1963).

Danto, Bruce L. (ed.). *Jail House Blues: Studies of Suicidal Behavior in Jail and Prison* (Orchard Lake, Mich.: Epic Publications, Inc., 1973).

Deutsch, M. "The Effects of Cooperation and Competition on Group Process," *Human Relations,* 2, 1949.

———. "Techniques of Inducing Cooperation Between Adversaries," Teachers College, Columbia, October 1, 1966.

Dizmang, Larry H., M.D. "Suicide Among the Cheyenne Indians," *Bulletin of Suicidology,* National Institute of Mental Health, Washington, D.C., July 1967.

Drucker, Peter. "The Psychology of Managing Management," *Psychology Today,* March 1968.

———. "There Are No Profit Centers . . . Only Cost Centers," *Harvard Business Review,* January–February 1968.

Durkheim, Emile. *Suicide* (New York: Free Press, 1951), p. 248.

Etzioni, Amatai. *A Comparative Analysis of Complex Organizations* (Glencoe, Ill.: Free Press, 1961).

———. *Modern Organizations* (Englewood Cliffs, N.J.: Prentice-Hall, 1964).

Ewalt, Jack R. *Facts About Mental Illness,* National Association of Mental Health, Washington, D.C., 1961.

Farberow, Norman L., and Edwin S. Schneidman (eds.). *The Cry for Help* (New York: McGraw-Hill, 1961).

Ferguson, Charles A. *A Legacy of Neglect* (Fort Worth: Industrial Mental Health Association, 1965).

Festinger, L. "A Theory of Social Comparison Process," *Human Relations,* 7, 1954.

Frank, Lawrence K. "The Promotion of Mental Health," *Mental Health in the United States,* The Annals of the American Academy of Political and Social Science, vol. 286, March 1963.

Friedlander, Frank. "Job Characteristics as Satisfiers and Dissatisfiers," *Journal of Applied Psychology,* 48, 1964.

Fromm, Erik. *The Sane Society* (New York: Reinhart, 1955).

Gardner, John W. *Self-Renewal, The Individual and the Innovative Society* (New York: Harper & Row, 1963).

Gellerman, Saul W. *Motivation and Productivity* (New York: American Management Association, 1963).

Goldiamond, Israel. "Moral Behavior: A Functional Analysis," *Psychology Today,* vol. 2, no. 4, September 1968.

Graves, Clare W. "Deterioration of Work Standards," *Harvard Business Review,* September–October 1966.

Greenblat, Milton, Richard H. York, and Esther Lucile Brown. *From Custodial to Therapeutic Patient Care in Mental Hospitals* (New York: Russell Sage, 1955).

Greiner, Larry E. "Patterns of Organizational Change," *Harvard Business Review,* May–June 1967.

Grollman, Earl A. *Suicide: Prevention, Intervention, Postvention* (Boston: Beacon Press, 1971).

Harvey, Jerry. "Some Dynamics of Intergroup Competition," *Training News,* vol. 8, nos. 3 and 4, Fall–Winter, 64–65, Washington.

Hatton, Corrine L., Sharon M. Valente, and Alice Rink. *Suicide: Assessment and Intervention* (New York: Appleton, 1977).

Henry, A., and J. Short, Jr. *Suicide and Homicide* (New York: Free Press, 1954).

Herman, Stanley M. *The People Specialists* (New York: Knopf, 1968), pp. 250–251.

Heron, Woodburn. "The Pathology of Boredom," *Frontiers of Psychological Research,* Stanley Coopersmith (ed.) (San Francisco: Freeman, 1964).

Herzberg, F., B. Mausner, and B. Schneiderman. *The Motivation to Work* (New York: Wiley, 1959).

Herzberg, Frederick. *Work and the Nature of Man* (Cleveland: World, 1966).

House, Robert J. *Management Development, Design, Evaluation and Implementation* (Ann Arbor: Bureau of Industrial Relations, 1967).

Hughes, Charles. *Goal Setting* (New York: American Management Association, 1965).

Kirkpatrick, Forrest H. "Guidelines for Management Development," *The Personnel Administrator,* July–August 1963.

Klagsbrun, Francine. *Youth and Suicide: Too Young to Die* (New York: Pocket Books, 1977).

Kobler, Arthur L., and Ezra Stotland. *The End of Hope, A Social-Clinical Study of Suicide* (Glencoe, Ill.: Free Press, 1964).

LeBold, William E. "Keeping Engineers Content," *Engineer,* July–August 1967.

Levine, S. "Stimulation in Infancy," *Scientific American,* 202, May 1960.

Levinson, Harry. *The Exceptional Executive* (Cambridge, Mass.: Harvard, 1968).

Liddell, Howard S. "Conditioning Emotions," *Scientific American,* January 1954.

Likert, Rensis. *New Patterns of Management* (New York: McGraw-Hill, 1961).

Litman, Robert E. "Emergency Response to Potential Suicide," *Journal of Michigan State Medical Society,* 62, January 1963.

Lorenz, Konrad. *On Aggression* (New York: Harcount, Brace & World, 1963).

Maier, Norman R. F. *Psychology in Industry* (New York: Houghton Mifflin, 1965).

Marshall, S. L. A. "Men Against Fire," *The Infantry Journal,* Washington, 1947.

Maslow, Abraham. *Eupsychian Management* (Homewood, Ill.: Irwin, 1955).

———. *Motivation and Personality* (New York: Harper & Brothers, 1954).

———. *Toward a Psychology of Being* (Princeton: Van Nostrand, 1962).

Masserman, Jules H. "Experimental Neurosis," *Scientific American,* March 1950.

Mayo, Elton. *The Social Problems of an Industrial Civilization* (Boston: Harvard Business School, 1945).

Mayor, William E., M.D. "Brainwashing," An address before the Freedom Foundation, Taft Broadcasting Company, Cincinnati.

McGee, Richard K. *Crisis Intervention in the Community* (Baltimore: University Park Press, 1974).

McGregor, Douglas. *The Human Side of Enterprise* (New York: McGraw-Hill, 1960).

Mechanic, David. *Psychological Stress* (St. Paul: University of Minnesota, 1930).

———. *Students Under Stress* (New York: Free Press, 1962).

Miller, William F. "Expert Finds Executives Inept at Job Hunting," *The Plain Dealer,* Sept. 2, 1968.

Neill, A. S. *Summerhill* (New York: Hart Publishing Company, 1964).

Olmstead, Joseph A. "The Skills of Leadership," *Military Review,* March 1967.

Pacifico, Carl. "Advice for Mismanagers," *Chemical and Engineering News,* vol. 46, no. 13, March 18, 1968.

Patton, Arch. "The Coming Scramble for Executive Talent," *Harvard Business Review,* May–June 1967.

Pepitone, Albert. "Self, Social Environment and Stress," in Mortimer Appley and Richard Trumbull (eds.), *Psychological Stress* (New York: Appleton, 1967).

Piel, Gerald. *Consumers of Abundance,* Center for the Study of Democratic Institutions, June 1961.

Presthus, Robert. *The Organizational Society* (New York: Knopf, 1962).

Pretzel, Paul W., *Understanding and Counseling the Suicidal Person* (New York: Abingdon, 1972).

Resnik, H. L. P. (ed.). *Suicidal Behaviors* (Boston: Little, Brown, 1968).

Sainsbury, Peter. *Suicides in London: An Ecological Study* (London: Chapman & Hall, 1955).

Satir, Virginia. *Conjoint Family Therapy* (Palo Alto: Science and Behavioral Books, Inc., 1964).

Schein, E. H., I. Schneier, and C. H. Barker. *Coercive Persuasion* (New York: Norton, 1961.

Schein, E. H. "Interpersonal Communication, Group Solidarity, and Social Influence," *Sociometry,* 1960.

———. *Organizational Psychology* (Englewood Cliffs, N.J.: Prentice-Hall, 1965).

Schutz, William C. "Interpersonal Underworld," *Harvard Business Review,* July–August 1958.

Scott, E. L. "Perceptions of Organization and Leadership Behavior," ONR Contr. N 6 ori-17 (Columbus: Ohio State University, 1952).

Selye, Hans. *The Stress of Life* (New York: McGraw-Hill, 1956).

Shepard, Herbert A. "Responses to Situations of Competition and Conflict," *Conflict Management in Organizations* (Ann Arbor: Foundation for Research in Human Behavior, 1961).

Sherif, Muzafer. "Experiments on Group Conflict and Cooperation," in Harold J. Leavitt and Louis R. Pondy (eds.), *Readings in Managerial Psychology* (Chicago: The University of Chicago Press, 1964).

Shils, E. H., and Janowitz, M. "Cohesion and Disintegration in the Wermacht in World War II," *Public Opinion Quarterly,* 12, 1948.

Schneidman, Edwin S., Norman L. Farberow, and Robert E. Litman (eds.), *The Psychology of Suicide* (New York: Science House, 1970).

Spitz, Rene. "Hospitalism: Genesis of Psychiatric Conditions in Early Childhood," *Psychoanalytic Study of the Child,* 1, 1945.

Stanton, Alfred H., and Morris S. Schwartz. *Mental Hospital* (New York: Basic Books, 1954).

Taylor, Frederick Winslow. *Scientific Management* (New York: Harper, 1911).

Torrance, E. P. "A Theory of Leadership and Interpersonal Behavior under Stress," in L. Petrullo and B. M. Bass (eds.), *Leadership and Interpersonal Behavior* (New York: Holt, 1961).

Van Egmond, Elmer, et al. "The Decision-Making Process in Self-Renewal," *American Journal of Orthopsychiatry.*

Varah, Chad (ed.). *The Samaritans* (New York: McMillan, 1965).

Waldman, Roy D., M.D. "Neurosis and the Social Structure," *American Journal of Orthopsychiatry,* vol. 38, no. 1, January 1968.

Wallace, Samuel E. *After Suicide* (New York: Wiley, 1973).

Whyte, William H., Jr. *The Organization Man* (Garden City, N.Y.: Doubleday, 1957).

Wolf, S., and H. A. Ripley. "Reactions Among Allied Prisoners of War Subjected to Three Years of Imprisonment and Torture by the Japanese," *American Journal of Psychiatry,* 104, 1944.

Zaill, Peter B. "Industrial Engineering and Socio-Technical Systems," *The Journal of Industrial Engineering,* vol. XVIII, no. 9, September 1957.

Zilboorg, Gregory. "Considerations on Suicide with Particular Reference to That of the Young," *American Journal of Orthopsychiatry,* 7, 1937.

Articles

"Analysis of the Omicron Company" (Ann Arbor: University of Michigan, 1964).

"Further Reflections on Conflict Management," *Conflict-Management in Organizations,* Elsie Boulding (ed.) (Ann Arbor: Foundation for Research in Human Behavior, 1961.

"Long Range Planning," *Business Management,* March 1967.

Index

Index